FOREWORD

A train and an interurban raced, on parallel tracks, across the Illinois countryside. The train maintained a steady pace, while the car feel behind at each passenger stop. But, as the train passenger, looking out the window, was about to dismiss the car from his mind, the relentless torque of trolley fed, series wound motors, applied to a sure-footed all wheel drive, would send the car charging ahead, only to be overtaken again at the next crossroads.

The city fell behind; hamlets were less frequent. The train increased its pace --- but not enough. Freed of numerous stops, the interurban pulled ahead; and disappeared in the distance.

This display of speed and acceleration was not lost upon Warren G. Brown, a young Kansas banker aboard the train. It was 1910 and steel rails were vital to the nation; but rail service was not without fault. A great need was for a better local train. The steam-powered local usually left the city in the morning and returned in the afternoon. The traveler took part of the first day to go to town, the second day to transact his business, and much of the third to return home. Two hotel bills were an extravagance, his clothes were filthy with coal soot, the neighbors had to milk the cows and it was durned inconvenient!

Contrary to a widely-held belief, the railroads were not running their trains that way to offend the public. At the end of its run a locomotive needs the services of a roundhouse staff. Before it can start steam must be raised. It can only operate out of central division points and, with four or more men to a crew, it takes a long, infrequent train, well-filled with passengers, to pay its way.

The interurban car could spend the night, unattended, anywhere on the line and, next morning, after ninety seconds to pump up air, it was off and away; powered by clean, unobtrusive electricity. Mr. Brown had seen an interurban which made its local stops and exceeded the speed of a mainline train. He had been approached to invest in a line to serve the Wichita, Kansas, area and it looked like a very sound investment.

Forty-four years later he said, "The Arkansas Valley Interurban was the saddest chapter in my life."

The interurban, which once held such promise, was a sad chapter in many lives. Fortunes were lost, employment was terminated and a way of life withered away.

*   *   *   *

Ira Swett's open house was sometimes called Swett Sunday evening Street Car Society. Or, flippantly, the Swett Shop. Most of us just called it Ira's. Each Sunday evening all traction fans were invited to meet at his home. Here was an opportunity to see each others' slides and movies, to study a basement full of transit industry publications and to meet with each other. This last was most informative. One could find specialists in all aspects of electric railroading.

And there was Ira himself. Big, genial, versitile: An athlete, musician, photographer, radio announcer, public relations director, author, publisher, historian and, most important to us; dean of the railfans. A generalist with much specialized knowledge.

On one of these pleasant occasions he asked if he would see me next week. The answer was no. I was going on vacation to Wichita, Kansas and, while there, I might be able to develop something on the Arkansas Valley Interurban. If I did, would he publish it? "Gladly!" And, in that informal, spur-of-the-moment way, Interurbans Special 19 was conceived.

A ten-day vacation with family and friends, can be all too swift without also undertaking a sizeable research effort. If one's father is an historian, it helps. Even so there was much still to learn when the vacation ended. This hopefully could be accomplished by correspondence. Progress was being made when the research and development project on which I was working suddenly became most demanding. Things weren't going right and every effort, by all hands, had to be expended to salvage the operation. This involved travel.

As a result, Special 19 was somewhat of a disappointment. It presents the general picture well enough but there were errors in detail and some things, which should have been included couldn't be learned at all, so they were omitted. Ira helped. His research, from his Magna Collection, answered questions which could have been answered in no other way. He prepared the section on cars and did some of the other writing as well. Without an energetic and long-suffering editor, Special 19 might have been years in preparation.

After two decades Special 19 is now reissued and we have taken the opportunity to correct old mistakes and to introduce new material. This time the work was undertaken without haste or pressure and the result is more satisfactory.

Even so, the reader should bear in mind that no human endeavor is ever perfect. Our sources have included old timers' memories which have been, at time, vague and sometimes have contradicted each other. The same is true of our written sources. Newspapers are the most available source of information but they are always prepared in haste and stories which are conflicting or sometimes unbelieveable appear now and then. Am example of an unbelieveable story appears in the 1910 "Transportation Issue" of the _Wichita Beacon_. An announcement states that an interurban terminal "like this one" will be built at the intersection of First and Water (see photo this page). The picture is a well-executed artist's likeness of the great Indianapolis Traction Terminal, nine tracks covered by a block-long trainshed, etc. The reality is the structure shown in the photo on this page.

If the reader finds something he believes to be wrong, hopefully he will drop us a line. Who knows? In another two decades we may undertake a complete revision, including a thorough rewrite for greater clarity and continuity. Of course we will include any newly-unearthed information and correct any new-found mistakes.

September 1977   Malcolm D. Isely

THE WICHITA TERMINAL (IN REALITY)

Readers of a 1910 edition of the Wichita Beacon _were told the new AVI terminal would be a palace; artists renderings of the great Indianapolis Traction Terminal, a nine-track trainshed-covered station were the illustration for the story. The small, plain structure above was what was actually constructed (see third column in "Foreword", above)._
-Dr. Edward N. Tihen

Above we see the driving of the first spike. Mayor Davidson of Wichita
and President W. O. Van Arsdale of AVI are seen driving the Silver
Spike in 1910. The Mayors of Kansas, who at the time of this ceremony
were attending the Mayors' Convention in Wichita, were guests.

Below is a photo of the construction train, borrowed from the Frisco
Railroad. Only the best oak ties and 70-lb. steel rails were used.
Standing at the extreme right is Mr. O. A. Boyle, then AVI's General
Manager. Next to him stands George Theis, Jr., Vice President.

Chapter 1

Prospectus

Arkansas Valley Interurban

AVI was a home-financed company. In order to raise funds for construction, it had to attract investment capital. To do this, an attractive forty page booklet was published. Well illustrated and in two colors, the booklet evidently accomplished its purpose, for sufficient monies were attracted to permit building the line.

In this chapter, we have selected pertinent pages from this prospectus for reproduction. Not only will they give the reader the flavor of those early AVI years, but they are instructive as well.

The front cover of the Prospectus is reproduced above.

Due to limitation on space, only nine pages of the prospectus are reproduced. However, almost all the illustrations are to be found in succeeding chapters, and the eight pages eliminated are of no great loss, having been given over to testimonials.   Thus the bulk of that original prospectus has been preserved herein; we hope you agree that it serves as a most interesting introduction to our Special 19.

The Prospectus was donated to the author by Miss Gracia Boyle, daughter of the late O. A. Boyle, AVI's first General Manager, and her generosity in making this valuable booklet available for reproduction is very much appreciated.

FOREWORD

IN PRESENTING this booklet to the public we have tried to give such points of information as will be of interest to the careful investor, together with views that will indicate the progress we are making in construction. We want this road to be a home enterprise—owned and controlled by the people of Kansas and the Arkansas Valley and their friends. ❡ We are confident this road will pay well, and we believe we are offering herein an exceptional opportunity for profitable investment. Look this booklet over carefully, study our proposition, and then let us have your co-operation in this great enterprise.

The Arkansas Valley Interurban Ry. Co.

OFFICERS

W. O. VAN ARSDALE, President

GEO. THEIS, Jr., Vice President

O. A. BOYLE, Vice President and General Manager

A. STONE, Secretary

E. T. BATTIN, Treasurer

R. L. HOLMES, General Attorney

DIRECTORS

W. O. VAN ARSDALE, President Van Arsdale-Osborne Brokerage Co.

GEO. THEIS, Jr., Capitalist.

C. G. COHN, Wallenstein & Cohn, Boston Store.

C. H. SMYTH, President Commercial Club, Smyth Storage Co.

D. C. ROUNDS, Rounds & Porter Lumber Co.

R. B. CAMPBELL, Capitalist.

E. T. BATTIN, Capitalist.

R. L. HOLMES, Holmes & Yankey, Attorneys,

O. A. BOYLE, President The Boyle Commission Co., Chamber of Commerce.

GEO. THEIS, Jr., Vice President
Capitalist

R. L. HOLMES, Gen. Attorney
Holmes & Yankey

E. T. BATTIN, Treasurer
Capitalist

A. STONE, Secretary
Sec'y Van Arsdale-Osborne
Brokerage Co.

O. A. BOYLE
Vice President and Manager

Pres. Boyle Commisson Co.
Pres. Chamber of Commerce

ORGANIZATION OF COMPANY

THE COMPANY was organized under the laws of the State of Kansas in 1903, for the purpose of operating a line of electric railway, providing rapid transit between Wichita, Hutchinson, Arkansas City, Wellington and intermediate towns in the Counties of Sedgwick, Harvey, Reno, Cowley and Sumner. The Company has the right of eminent domain and power to carry on all forms of railroad business.

CAPITALIZATION

Stock (all common) authorized, $2,100,000.00.
  To be issued on basis of the actual cost of road, complete,
  ready for operation.
Bonds authorized
  To be issued on basis of the actual cost of road, complete,
  ready for operation.

FRANCHISES

Franchises have been and are being secured in the towns and on the public highways in the counties through which the road passes.

RIGHT-OF-WAY

The road is being constructed on private right-of-way from sixty-six to eighty feet wide, which is sufficient width for double tracks when necessary.

RIGHT-OF-WAY

HE HIGHEST modern standards are being adopted in the construction of this line with a special view to permanence and low cost of maintenance. It is upon private right-of-way and will operate under long time franchises through the towns. The grades and alignment are particularly favorable and will enable operation at a high rate of speed, in competition with steam roads. Steel and reinforced concrete bridges will be constructed across all streams of consequence and substantial culverts will be placed at all necessary points.

CONSTRUCTION

Work on the grading and construction of the road is progressing rapidly. The road is now being completed to Sedgwick, a distance of seventeen and one-half miles from Wichita.

CONSTRUCTIVE FEATURES

Right-of-way fenced with Osage Posts 16' apart with four strands of Galvanized Barbed Wire or American hog tight fencing. Small culverts vitrified sewer pipe. All important bridges concrete and steel. No. 1, 6" x 8" x 8' White Oak Ties, 70 lb. A. S. C. E. Standard Steel "T" rails. Duquesne or 100% joints, which have been recently adopted as standard on the Pennsylvania R. R. and are fast being adopted by other steam roads as well as Electric roads. Electrically bonded with 4-0 Twin Terminal Bonds. Cross Bonded every 1000'. Poles for overhead and Transmission lines 50' Western Cedar with 8" tops. Transmission wires No. 2 Copper strand. Trolley Wire 4-0 grooved Copper suspended on No. 1 "C" Tubing flexible pole brackets. Feeder Wire 4-0 round Copper placed on a 5' cross arm with two No. 12 Copper Telephone Wires. Lightning arresters on every ninth pole.

Private Telephone system connecting the dispatcher's office with all depots, switches, and sub stations, also portable phones on all cars.

High Tension Circuit three phase 60c ycle, 33000 volts. Motor Generator sub stations twelve miles apart, converting power from 33000 A. C. to 600 volts D. C. Sub stations fireproof, brick construction.

If you are not familiar with Electric Railway Construction submit the above data to any one who is and get their judgment.

CARS

Orders have been placed for combination passenger, smoker and baggage cars of the highest standard interurban type. They are being especially constructed from plans which are designed to meet the particular requirements of this road. They will be equipped with automatic air brakes, heavy trucks, automatic couplers and four sixty-five H. P. motors each, enabling them to operate at a high rate of speed. The cut of the beautiful car on the cover is a photograph of car No. 1, just arrived.

TERRITORY SERVED

The line will operate northward from Wichita through Valley Center, Sedgwick, Newton, Halstead, Burrton and Hutchinson. These towns are well located along the route of the line with no other interurban road serving them.

The road will serve one hundred thousand people, including the termini.

The rural districts are well settled. The people are prosperous and every foot of land is tillable, and, with intensified farming, four families will live where there is now one.

The road will develop the dairy business as well as truck farming.

WHY SHOULD YOU INVEST

IN THE BONDS OF THE ARKANSAS VALLEY INTERURBAN RAILWAY

FIRST. Your money is absolutely safe, being secured by a First Mortgage on all the property of this road now owned or shall hereafter be acquired in Cowley, Sumner, Reno, Harvey and Sedgwick Counties.

SECOND. You have a guaranteed income of six per cent. payable semi-annually. Interest begins the day your money is paid.

THIRD. By subscribing now you also get a bonus of stock free, amounting to 25 per cent. of the amount of bonds you buy.

FOURTH. Other Interurbans now in Kansas are making big profits. One line which cost $5,000.00 per mile more than ours, and which has an average population per mile about one half as great as that along the Arkansas Valley Interurban, made 9 ½ per cent. net the second year, after cost of operation, taxes, insurance, and interest on the bonds were paid, and 11 ½ per cent. in the third year.

FIFTH. Now suppose that we, with a much larger population and with a much cheaper road should earn only 6 per cent. in the second year. Certainly your stock would be worth at least par, and here is what your investment shall bring you in return at that time.

$250.00 worth of stock at par $250.00
Interest on $1,000.00 worth of bonds at 6 per cent. [for two years] 120.00
6 per cent. earnings on $250.00 worth of stock 15.00
Total, $385.00

This is figured on the basis of an investment of $1,000.00 in these bonds, and according to this estimate would net you above 19 per cent. per annum. The same would be true for an investment of any amount.

SIXTH. We are using the best and most modern equipment in building this road, yet cost of construction is at a minimum since there are no expensive cuts or fills on the grade, and no bridges or trestles worthy of mention.

SEVENTH. Our line traverses one of the most fertile valleys on the face of the globe, every foot of the soil of which is capable of the highest cultivation.

EIGHTH. This is a home enterprise, built and controlled by the people of the Arkansas Valley. You have the advantage of knowing the business reputation of every officer and director, and of being right here where you can see how every dollar of your money is being spent.

NINTH. This road will mean more to Wichita and to the other towns and communities served by this road than any other enterprise now under consideration. It is sure to enchance property values all along the line, and by helping build this road you are making more valuable all your other holdings in the Arkansas Valley.

TENTH. Farmers, laboring men, professional men, business men, and twenty-two of the best bankers in Southern Kansas have bought a portion of these bonds. They are issued in denominations as small as one hundred dollars, so if you can spare no more you can take advantage of this opportunity for profitable investment just the same as you could if you had ten thousand dollars

ELEVENTH. You should not delay this matter but should send in your subscriptions today before the bonus stock offer is withdrawn. And keep in mind the three points which characterize this investment—*absolute safety, a guaranteed income, and big profits.*

Turn to the subscription blank, fill it out, and send to us by return mail.

Send all inquiries to O. A. Boyle, General Manager, Tenth Floor, Beacon Building, Wichita, Kansas.

In the above photo the cleared right-of-way of AVI is seen paralleling the Santa Fe Railway; for almost three miles just south of Valley Center the interurban and steam lines were cheek by jowl. AVI boasted that "We will rival the limited trains of the steam road in speed; while for ease, comfort, cleanliness and convenience the electric road is 'The Only Way.'"

Below, eighteen cars of steel and other equipment for the AVI are shown being unloaded in AVI's material yards at Valley Center in 1910. While this activity proceeded, forty more cars of construction material for the Valley Center-Sedgwick segment were arriving, and another trainload was on the way. Busy days, indeed!

Wichita, Kansas, is located at the confluence of the Big and Little Arkansas Rivers (which, in the state of Kansas, is pronounced "Ar-Kan-Sas", and in the state of Arkansas is pronounced Ar-Kan-Saw --like the state itself) and is named for the Wichita Indians who first settled there. The indians found fertile soil, abundant water and groves of giant cottonwoods. As central Kansas goes the area is scenic. The flat riverbottom gives way to low, rolling hills to the east.

The first whites were indian traders who built permanent trading posts and established a reputation for honest dealing. This attracted other "white people" of similar outlook. In a lawless time and place Wichita became a haven for those who made their livelihood by industry rather than by predatoriness. Before Wyatt Earp became Marshall of Dodge City he was fired from his job as Wichita's dog catcher. Wichita was a peaceable, orderly place. It had no Boot Hill.

But Wichita also had no railroad. Those scenic heights, east of town, were a bar to railroad construction. Santa Fe's Grand Canyon route and Rock Island's Golden State route cross at Hutchinson, where the land is flat as a billiard table. Wichita people built their own rail connection and sold it to the Santa Fe.

Only the Frisco came in from the east. We have observed Frisco freights creeping up the reverse curve between Ninth and 17th Sts., going ever more slowly until the locomotive, like some living thing shrugging off an intolerable burden, would spin its wheels, throw the fire up the stack and quit. All this within the Wichita yard limit. Perhaps because of the grades the Frisco was an early user of electric traction. Its GE gas-electric cars climbed the grade with ease until they were abandoned when the Frisco was nationalized in 1917.

But, like Los Angeles without a good, natural harbor, Wichita thrived anyway. By 1903 ,when the Arkansas Valley Interurban was incorporated, it was the second largest city in Kansas: a milling, meat packing and wholesaling center. It was the home of Mentholatum and of Coleman Lamps (both nationally known) and there were numerous other factories. Wichita had great visions of its own future, calling itself the *Peerless Princess of the Plains*. But, in an era when railroads were vitrually the only means of intercity travel, it had rather ordinary rail service.

There were through trains from Wichita to Topeka, Kansas City and Chicago; but Newton had more. There were through trains to Oklahoma City, Dallas-Ft. Worth and the Gulf; but Winfield had more. Hutchinson had through trains to Denver, Colorado Springs, El Paso, Phoenix and San Francisco. Wichita had none. We cannot determine whether or not Wichita had a through train to Los Angeles (by way of Woodward and Amarillo) but we know that Hutchinson had several.

Seven years later, when the AVI was built, it located its stations across the street from the Santa Fe depots in Newton and Hutchinson but, even though a modern Union Station was being built in Wichita, the AVI never bothered to locate near it. Wichita's interurban terminal was in the heart of the shopping district. People came to Wichita to *shop*. They went to *Newton* and *Hutchinson* to catch a train. Thus the AVI had the usual sources of interurban business plus a considerable number of passengers who went from Wichita to outlying towns because of the superior railroad service there. An unusual and profitable circumstance, indeed.

The AVI was the only intercity rail carrier with its headquarters in Wichita and its Ackerman's Island shops were one of two complete overhaul shops for railroad equipment in Wichita. (The Kansas City, Mexico & Orient maintained a locomotive back shop there, having been subsidized by the city of Wichita in the amount of $30,000 to do so.) Wichita, which is now Kansas' largest city, is still not a major railroad center.

On June 10, 1903, the Kansas State Charter Board chartered the AVI. Of the 17 directors, six were from towns south of Wichita. Some of these had no railroad and desired one very much (later the Midland Valley served these areas).

At the first director's meeting O. A. Boyle was elected president and, for the next ten years, he was closely identified with the AVI and seemed to be its principal promoter. His daughter, Miss Gracia Boyle, told of many childhood trips over the AVI with her father, as he traveled to attend to its affairs. W. O. Van Arsdale succeeded him as president at the same time the line was built, but Boyle then became president of the AVI construction company which built, and partly financed, the line.

When the AVI was finally built, it went *north*, not south from Wichita. The first segment, from Wichita to Sedgewick, was financed by A. A. Hyde, O. A. Boyle, the Wichita *Eagle*, Henry Schweiter and others who subscribed $50,000, on March 3, 1910.

2,100 shares of common stock were authorized at $100 par, but it is doubtful that any ever sold at par. The original investors received free common stock in the amount of 25% of the value of the bonds they purchased. In July of 1955, Warren. G. Brown told us that he had always valued his entire holding of AVI common at $1.00. Brown was Board Chairman of Brown Cummer & Co. and a director of the Santa Fe Railway. He doubtless knew what AVI common was worth.

This is not to say that there was anything dishonest about the building of the AVI. This was well within the mores of the time and there was no hint of waste, corruption, mismanagement or misrepresentation in the AVI's affairs. The company was clean; like the rest of Wichita.

$1,500,000 in preferred stock was authorized of which $499,990 was issued. $3,000,000 worth of 6% bonds were authorized and $856,000 worth were sold.

The city of Wichita gave the AVI sixty $500 bonds of the city, maturing in 20 years and drawing 4% interest. The AVI then sold the bonds, with a par value of $30,000, and used the money to build a station and buy real estate in Wichita. A 2/3rd majority of the voters was required to pass a bond issue and, in the election held on May 3, 1910, 2,113 favored the bonds and 522 opposed them.

The AVI also received a $30,000 grant from Hutchinson and friends of Bethel College raised $20,000 by private subsbcription to build the local line to Bethel. Newton never made a grant to the AVI but the AVI asked Newton investors to subscribe $100,000 to buy AVI bonds and apparently they did. At least the line was built into Newton.

The merchants of Newton and Hutchinson tended to look askance at the AVI. It seemed to them that frequent interurban service to Wichita would cause many of their patrons to go there, where the larger retail stores offered a greater variety. The Hutchinson *Gazette* maintained an editorial policy opposing

the AVI on the grounds that it would be "bad for business" in Hutchinson. Unlike the merchants, the people of Newton and Hutchinson favored the AVI and made great use of its services.

On July 22, 1913, W. O. Van Arsdale refused a fourth term as president, saying that George Theis, Jr., now owned a controlling interest in the AVI the should assume that duty. O. A. Boyle, who had sold most of his common stock to Theis, resigned as president of the construction company although he remained a director of the AVI. Theis was elected and, like Flagler of the Florida East Coast, Moffat of the Denver & Salt Lake or Spreckels of the San Diego & Arizona, began trying to extend the AVI.

It was not doing well financially and interurbans generally were regarded as poor investment. However, he saw a need for the AVI and, like Boyle before him, began trying to fill the need. On January 18, 1915, Theis spoke to the commercial club of Hutchinson. He said that the AVI was earning $140,000 a year and meeting expenses, including interest at 6% on the bonds. He also said that, of the $856,000 in bonds which had been issued, that $350,000 were still held by the AVI construction company. He added that it would take an additional $300,000 to build into Hutchinson but, he expected, that the line would be able to pay dividends if only the Hutchinson extension could be built.

Theis was right about the Hutchinson extension putting the AVI solidly in the black but it never paid any dividends. It did retire $526,300 worth of bonds but there was always a new investment need, principally the Wichita relocation, which was given priority for any surplus. Boyle, Theis and the others didn't plan it that way. They hoped to make money but, when they did not, they kept trying, to the end, to give the best service possible whether the line paid or not. Like Boyle, Theis seemed to take a sort of evangelical approach to the AVI. He was a Methodist Sunday school teacher and his entire class made an excursion to Hutchinson and back soon after the Hutchinson extension opened.

Wichita's two suppliers of electricity and its streetcars came under the unified management of the Kansas Gas & Electric Co. in 1910. In that year KG&E built the Wichita plant, which had four 550-volt 500KVA motor-generator sets driven from the 2,300-volt A.C. alternators (no transformers) in the same building. These supplied Wichita's streetcars, operated by KG&E's wholly owned streetcar subsidiary, the Wichita Railroad & Light Co., several downtown office buildings with D.C. elevators, KG&E's coal car shunting trolley locomotive and the AVI as far north as 29th St.

Beyond 29th St. the AVI provided its own 600-volt direct current from its Valley Center and Van Arsdale substations. These drew power from KG&E's new 60,000-volt high tension line and the AVI and KG&E arranged for a joint right-of-way for the interurban and the pole line. Thus the AVI subs were right on the high line and the AVI attached its bracket arms to KG&E poles most of the way. The poles were 50 feet high, two feet in diameter at the base and 110 feet apart. The vertical alignment of the poles was so nearly perfect that a person standing between two poles could look in either direction and see only the first pole. All others would be hidden by it.

The AVI erected a two-story brick substation

In the above view, the graders are shown changing the channel
of Jcster Creek in 1910. The old bed was filled to avoid a
long curve at this point. By changing the channel, AVI track
was given an absolute straight line between Valley Center and
Sedgwick. Note the small scrapers used.

Below we see the newly completed interurban line at a point
near Valley Center. This gives a good idea of the large
poles used and their excellent alignment. Kansas Gas &
Electric Company's transmission line shared this pole line
with AVI's trolley system.

a mile south of Valley Center. Trolley wire was No. 0000, and a 0000 feeder ran the complete length of the line. Untreated oak ties without plates, seventy pound rail, and soil ballast completed the picture. This construction was more than adequate for the service anticipated and was considered quite substantial for an interurban of that day.

Grading was done by men with teams and slip scrapers. The land was essentially flat and low areas along the Little Arkansas River were subject to flooding. Knowing this, Engineer Chas. D. Bell had the course of Jester Creek changed so that the cars could operate safely, in a straight line, between Valley Center and Sedgwick. Years later Jester Creek played a very bad joke on AVI; it got out of its man made channel and washed out a mile of track. That should not detract, however, from the feat of moving the creek channel, two cubic feet at a time, with animal power.

AVI selected a site at the corner of First & Water Streets in downtown Wichita for the location of its temporary station facilities. The location was in the heart of the city and all local streetcars passed within a half block of it. When increased traffic demanded it, AVI's proprietors planned to erect a more fitting station structure. Also in Wichita was the new $750,000 power plant of KG&E, one of the finest plants in the west and source of AVI's power.

To reach its Wichita station, AVI cars had to operate over the tracks of the Wichita Railway & Light Company. AVI's track met the WR&L track at 21st & Market Streets, with the interurbans running downtown from there over the local company's Stock Yards car route. WR&L double tracked and strengthened the line from 14th St. north to 21st St. Streetcar traffic on this particular line was heavy and AVI had to make it from 21st St. to downtown in less than twelve minutes if the interurban were to compete with the Santa Fe's running time from Valley Center.

After the tracks to Valley Center were laid and surfaced, the track-laying gangs continued northward to Sedgwick, 6.5 miles north of Valley Center and 17.8 miles out of Wichita. The work of laying rails over this portion of the line began in September.

The AVI's new track was physically connected with the WR&L Stock Yards line on October 15, 1910, at 21st & Market Streets. Early in the morning a few days thereafter, a special pre-inaugural inspection trip to Valley Center was made in two WR&L streetcars. In the party were AVI officials, Wichita businessmen, city officials, and reporters; the trip was made without mishap in thirty five minutes.

Eight new combination passenger & baggage cars, with green mohair seats and stained arch windows, had been ordered from St. Louis Car Company---which closed down for reorganization before delivery could be made. So, two other cars, appropriately numbered One and Two, were obtained and brought to Valley Center, arriving two weeks apart in November.

On Saturday morning, November 19, 1910, the official public opening of the line to Valley Center was celebrated. Car No. One left the Beacon Building, Wichita, at 9:30, its air whistle gloriously tooting a salute to the new era of fast, comfortable electric transportation. Tracks to Sedgwick from Valley Center had been laid by this time, and as soon as the big green car came to a halt at Valley Center, end of the trolley wire, a Frisco switch engine from the construction train was coupled to the car and chuffed northward to Sedgwick. The opening of the first segment of the AVI was a grand occasion for all and was met with unanimous approval along the entire line. Farmers stopped work in the fields and their wives and children came out to watch the speeding interurban car; even the cows and horses seemed surprised to behold the old dream finally come true. That afternoon at two o'clock the first regular cars were run to Valley Center, running on a two hour headway until ten at night.

The Interurban Construction Company was the affiliated company which actually built the AVI. Its officers were names familiar in AVI's officer roster: O. A. Boyle, George Theis, Jr., and others.

With two cars in service, AVI hired four crews, two shifts for each car. The first fou? motormen were: J. H. Anderson, T. H. Griffith, Robert Biles, and W. A. Faulkner. Two conductors had been selected: T. H. Walker and a Mr. Strong. President Boyle of the Construction Company reported that while in Valley Center that day a creamery man from that town had looked him up and had booked passage for one and one-half tons of milk and cream for the first AVI car into Wichita the following Monday morning, November 21st. Thus began AVI's freight business. AVI charged a 25¢ fare to Valley Center from Wichita; this may perhaps be considered to have been quite a travel bargain for was not the luxurious smoking compartment of Car No. One actually finished in real leather? To cap the AVI birth announcement that day was a banner across the top of the "Beacon's" front page exclaiming in big type: "Shake, Valley Center, Both Of Us Are To Be Congratulated."

Electrification of the Valley Center to Sedgwick segment was completed by December 17th, and again a special car carrying high company officials made an inspection trip, this time arriving in Sedgwick without the aid of the steam locomotive. Running time from the heart of Wichita was one hour.

<u>BUILDING TO NEWTON & HALSTEAD:</u> Further construction of the interurban ceased during the winter months and the time was devoted to furthering the sale of AVI stock and bonds in the vicinity of Newton, 11.7 miles north of Sedgwick and 29.5 miles from Wichita. AVI asked $100,000 worth of support from Newton individuals but only about two-thirds of the amount had been raised by the end of November, 1910. A few Newton business men were reported to be hesitant about investing in the AVI, fearing that the line would ultimately turn out to be a Wichita-to-Hutchinson project with only an unimportant branch line to serve Newton. On December 1st the controversy reached fever pitch when AVI officials issued an ultimatum to the people of Newton: "No $100,000---No Interurban!" Newton's Mayor threw the interurban question squarely into the laps of the people by calling a special election April 25th, 1911, to decide whether or not Newton did want the electric connection to Wichita. The election was held and resulted in an overwhelming victory for AVI: 689 to 26. Three days later the Newton city fathers gave AVI its franchise and company officials at once let contracts for the necessary material to extend from Sedgwick into Newton.

By late April a camp called "Interurbanville" had been set up five miles southwest of Newton hard by the Santa Fe's double track Chicago-California main line where AVI was to build a $15,000 viaduct over the steam tracks. Grading from Sedgwick to the viaduct site was completed by the end of April, there being no earth-moving difficulties encountered across the flat prairie land. AVI construction men tackled the high viaduct with energy: some 50,000 cubic yards of earth would have to be moved to carry the AVI main line 26 feet above the Santa Fe main line. A total of 45 teams and 66 men worked on the grading, while 25 teams and 44 men worked on the concrete abutments; the latter were to support a 40-foot-long metal span of bridge beams. After finishing the viaduct approaches the graders found it easy to cover the remaining five miles into Newton, and arrived there in early June, 1911.

On June 27th, AVI officials reported the line had been completed to a point six miles from Newton and that the two story brick substation at the Rebstock School was almost finished; this structure was later renamed Van Arsdale, in honor of AVI's first president, and became the junction of the Newton Division and the Wichita-Hutchinson main line.

The AVI construction train steamed up W. Fifth St. into Newton on Thursday, September 28th, and the first interurban car reached Newton's Main Street under its own power on Monday, October 9th. The following day the Wichita "Beacon" exclaimed: "Howdy, Newton. Now We Are Much Closer Neighbors." It took the cars two hours to make the run, but the public was promised faster time later. The first passenger car to run from Wichita to Newton by electricity left Wichita at 2:00 PM Tuesday, October 10th; on board were AVI

officers and directors making their official inspection of the new line. First regular passenger service was established with the car leaving Wichita at 5:00 AM Wednesday, October 11th; a fare of 65¢ was established for the 29½ mile trip.

Newton went all out to celebrate the coming of the AVI. Tuesday, October 24th, was the big day, and more than two hundred Wichita business men rode the interurbans to be present. A special platform was built for the dignitaries just off Main Street in downtown Newton. A civic parade in the morning and an electric parade at night were staged, while bands from Halstead, McPherson and Wichita played throughout the day.

The Newton station was originally in a brick office building on E. 5th St. adjacent to the Santa Fe depot; later it was moved to a modest one story brick building a block west---containing a waiting room, ticket office, baggage room, and freight offices.

<u>THE HUTCHINSON EXTENSION:</u> Immediately following the completion of the line into Newton, construction crews began working straight west from Van Arsdale Junction, the location of the second substation. This extension was built into the city of Halstead, five miles from the junction and 28.5 miles from Wichita. The first cars began regular operation early in the fall of 1911 and for several years this constituted the total mileage of AVI---29.5 miles of main line from Wichita to Newton, plus five additional miles from Van Arsdale Jct. to Halstead.

The ultimate goal of AVI's promoters was the thriving city of Hutchinson, 24 miles west of Halstead, with its salt mines, flour mills and the gateway to the great plains of Southwest Kansas. However, a combination of difficulties and complexities succeeded in keeping AVI out of Hutchinson for almost four more years.

Hutchinson buzzed with electric interurban schemes in the years following 1910, AVI being only one of the many proposals. They all came to naught, however, with the single exception of the Hutchinson & Northern, an electric switching line serving steam roads and industries in East Hutchinson since the early 1900s; the H&N had visions of grandeur as an interurban line but all remained paper dreams. Local electric railway service in Hutchinson was provided by the Hutchinson Interurban Railway Company. Sometime in 1914, Vice-president Theis of AVI and HI's President Emerson Carey signed an agreement providing for the entrance of AVI cars into Hutchinson over the streetcar company's tracks; HI extended its line one mile east of the Larabee Flour Mill in East Hutchinson to hook up with the AVI's right of way.

Theis, after considerable difficulty, at length succeeded in raising sufficient funds to permit construction work to resume. The eastern financiers "laughed at me," reported Theis later, "so it was up to us to dig down into our own pockets. The men in this project have made some great sacrifices in putting the road through. We have been forced to dispose of other holdings in order to raise the money for this line. But we have it. Every cent of the $1,200,000 now invested in AVI has been put up by men in the company and by cities along the line."

Construction work began in April, 1915, only to be halted for weeks at a time by right of way difficulties and by heavy rains (which alone caused an added expense of $25,000). The Rock Island gave AVI a bit of trouble by prohibiting the interurban from crossing its main line at grade; this was resolved only after AVI promised to install a crossing gate. A substation was erected at Burrton, midway on the new line; this was one of the most unique substation buildings to be found anywhere: it was built of glass and tapestry brick and was designed to contain depot facilities; when illuminated at night, it presented an unusually spectacular appearance.

On June 22, 1915, AVI purchased a depot site in downtown Hutchinson on E. 2nd Ave. between Walnut and Poplar, one and a half

Above we see the first passenger cars from Wichita arriving in Newton. The date was October 11, 1911, and the cars are No. 6 in foreground and No. 3 in rear. This shows Main St., looking north from 5th St. The photo was loaned by Miss Gracia Boyle, daughter of AVI's Vice President, Mr. O. A. Boyle.

Below is a lineup of AVI cars just outside Hutchinson on the opening day of through service from Wichita, December 20th, 1915. From left to right are cars 6, 201, 7 and 5. Note un-ballasted condition of track; very little of AVI's track was ever ballasted, unfortunately. (RJA)

When AVI's interurbans reached Hutchinson in 1915, they shared city tracks with these little single truckers of the Hutchinson Interurban Railway. In this 1909 view, taken at Main St. & Ave. A, six HI cars are shown posed with their crews. Note Brill semi-convertible at left, built by American in 1906, and the St. Louis car at extreme right with Dupont No. 3 truck.   (Floyd Harrison Photo)

blocks east of Main Street. Here AVI built a pretentious two story brick station. At about this time it completed its trackage westward to the Larabee Mills where it tied in with the Ave. A line of HI, which the big green interurbans were to use to get downtown to Main St., thence running two blocks north to 2nd Ave. for the swing east to the depot.

Much of AVI's new track was laid in 80-lb. and 90-lb. second hand steam railroad rails which Theis picked up at bargain prices; it was said that he saved $50,000 to $75,000 by this procedure.

On Monday, December 20, 1915, the first AVI car rolled into Hutchinson, touching off a gigantic celebration. The official entry must have been impressive: a car of the HI bearing city officials, reporters and other dignitaries, proceeded some eight miles eastward before meeting the six AVI cars from Wichita, laden with hundreds of visitors. The little streetcar then escorted the interurbans back into Hutchinson "in a triumphal procession such as will never again be witnessed in this city," to quote the Hutchinson "Gazette." Representing AVI at the civic reception which crammed three thousand excited people into the Con-

vention Hall were President Theis, Vice President Van Arsdale, Treasurer Smyth, as well as Mayor Bentley of Wichita. Two days later the first regular passenger car whistled in Hutchinson bearing Mr. L. B. Davis of Newton, the initial paying customer. The first schedule called for 13 runs daily, leaving Hutchinson and Wichita at identical times: 6:40, 8:00, 9:20, 10:40, 12:00 noon, 1:20, 2:40, 4:00, 5:20, 6:40, 8:00, 9:20 and 11:00 PM. The 13 car daily schedule from Newton to Van Arsdale Jct. was listed as 6:15, 6:25, 7:30, 8:50, 10:45, 12:05, 1:25, 2:45, 4:05, 5:06, 6:26, 7:46, and 9:06. The trip from Hutchinson to Wichita required two hours and 20 minutes. One daily freight train was also operated from Hutchinson to Wichita and return, with rail connections made to three steam roads at Hutchinson, with the Frisco at Burrton and more interchange tracks to be installed at Wichita. On December 28, 1915, AVI's phone line was completed into Hutchinson and the dispatching station was set up on Lorraine St. near the Rock Island crossing; here AVI trainmen received instructions to proceed east to the next phone station at Burrton. Eventually an AVI dispatcher was installed in the Hutchinson depot. As a prophecy of what was to come, AVI within a month of its opening was hauling a good amount of salt

out of Hutchinson---giving the steam roads a little competition.

Thus AVI acquired its full growth. As a full fledged interurban system, it boasted twelve passenger motor cars, two passenger trailers, three motor express cars, two locomotives and numerous freight cars. It could have advantageously used a better power distribution system, more ballast and faster schedules, but these never were realized.

In July, 1929, the Hutchinson Station yard was inundated, as this photo shows.

The Bethel Line

Although Newton was somewhat apathetic to the AVI, Bethel College, a mile north of Newton, was very desirous of obtaining service into Newton. Bleak was the campus in those days which did not boast a trolley line. Fairmount, Friends, Southwestern and nearly every other college in the area was served by streetcars. Bethel authorities felt that lack of good public transportation was indeed a serious disadvantage.

President Kliewer of Bethel, in his report to the annual college corporation meeting in 1912, called attention to this problem. The natural solution seemed to be the extension of the recently completed AVI line through Newton to the Bethel campus. R. A. Goerz, a director of the college, actively sponsored such an extension. Newspapers joined the crusade and plans soon began to take concrete form. By the middle of January, 1913, the sum of $20,000 had been subscribed by Bethel friends for the AVI extension to the campus.

In spite of some difficulties regarding the right of way, an agreement was reached in February, 1913, between the County Commissioners, the property owners, and the AVI. This agreement located the right of way along the east side of the road between Newton and the college, and assured the building of the line. Work began at once and was energetically pushed by both AVI and the Newton promoters. The line was completed early in the fall of 1913 and the first run was made on the evening of October 25th. Three cars carried AVI officials, the Newton Commercial Band, leading merchants of Newton, and friends of the college to a short inaugural program given on the front steps of the Main Building; Bethel was represented by President Kliewer, and AVI had as its spokesman Mr. O. A. Boyle, its President.

On December 1st an entertainment was given in the College Chapel in honor of the donors of right of way and the inauguration of car service; the program featured organ music, readings, vocal solos, and messages from the college and AVI official families.

Inasmuch as the college line would not require a large car, AVI purchased a single truck, closed, thirty-foot city car which it numbered 51. Bravely little 51 entered on the task of connecting Bethel and Newton. In spite of repeated schedule changes, the time schedule failed to give satisfaction either to the patrons from the point of view of service, or to the railway company from the point of view of financial income. AVI made some effort to provide a more attractive service by purchasing a Birney (AVI No. 100) in 1921 but receipts consistently failed to meet expenses. Service was dropped completely during vacation periods and after the final classes each day.

In November, 1920, AVI petitioned the State Court of Industrial Relations for permission to abandon the extension. This was denied but the company came back again in 1922 and again was rejected. In April, 1923, the Kansas Public Utilities Commission, which now had jurisdiction, ruled that service must continue. The company immediately asked the Federal Court for an injunction restraining the PUC from enforcing its order on the grounds that the order was unreasonable, unjust, oppressive and in violation of the U.S. Constitution. The court found for the company and the city now appealed. Finally, on October 27, 1925, with the case pending before the U.S. Supreme Court, AVI quietly signed an agreement with the city providing for abandonment with AVI paying all removal, repaving and litigation costs. The Bethel Line was officially abandoned on November 1, 1925, and on the following day the work of removing rails began. AVI sold the Birney to the Union Electric Railway of Coffeyville.

So ended a line which was minor but unique: it was AVI's only operation of a strictly local type. The Bethel Line was a social asset as well as a utility to the college; students and faculty met, informally, on the tiny car which, with the interurbans, was in demand to move students and friends to and from any of the numerous functions of the school year.

AVI interurban No. 10 is seen here on the Bethel College campus about 1913. In the background may be seen the imposing Bethel College Administration Building. (BC)

An AVI interurban crosses the N. Main St. bridge in Newton about 1916. The bridge carried vehicular traffic over Sand Creek. (BC)

Here is a poor photograph of an AVI rented city car and an interurban of the 3-10 Class at Bethel College. The photo was copied from a small photo in a college annual. This city car probably was relieving 51.

GROWTH & RETRENCHMENT: The AVI expanded its services and, within limits, prospered. Additional rolling stock was acquired. On August 12, 1916, a telephone dispatcher system was put in service. Small wooden phone booths appeared at sidings and motormen thus were brought within constant reach of the dispatcher. AVI was not nationalized in World War I but, with the price of copper at 23¢ a pound, people stole rail bonds out of the track and sold them to unscrupulous junk dealers. They even tore down charged trolley wire over sidings.

Plans for a northern extension to Salina had first taken the form of acquiring the existing Missouri Pacific branch from Newton to McPherson (30 miles) and a Union Pacific branch from McPherson into Salina (35 miles); however, first MOP refused to sell its branch without selling the entire line to ElDorado as well; AVI felt it could not operate the latter successfully and so turned down the deal. Later the ElDorado oil fields came in and AVI missed the boat again. This was in 1915; again in 1922 the matter came up anew, but President Theis held off due to increased auto competition.

By 1920 the automobile, which was even faster than the streetcar, had become well established as a means of personal transportation. In metropolitan areas, where streets were generally paved, it constituted genuine competition to the latter. The local systems of Wichita and Hutchinson suffered and the one urban operation of AVI (the Bethel line) became more of a liability than ever. This operation was abandoned (see page 16) but this did not mean that AVI was declining. It was simply retrenchment in an area where the company no longer planned to operate. Plans for the Salina line were still being actively pursued with the southern branches also back under consideration. An informal agreement had been reached about 1920 with the Oklahoma Railway which called for AVI to build south to South Haven on the Kansas-Oklahoma line, while the Oklahoma Railway would build north from Guthrie to South Haven. This link between Oklahoma City and Wichita would doubtless have been profitable at the time. One could then have ridden from Newton to Norman and, with a short gap to Sherman, Texas, could then have continued on to Waco or Corsicana on the Texas Electric. An interurban empire was in the making.

About $300,000 was spent in 1921 building a new interurban terminal and shops in Wichita; see "Facilities" chapter.

AUTOMOBILE & BUS: City lines had been hard hit by the automobile before World War I but, until the mid-'20s, the auto was too unreliable, expensive and uncomfortable for long distance travel. The principal drawback lay in the roads which were either dusty or muddy and always rutted. When a short auto ride could take one to the interurban station it was folly to drive a long distance to the city, yet during the Twenties the growing passenger business of the AVI was arrested. The population and prosperity of the area continued to grow by leaps and bounds, but with prosperity came improved rural roads. In 1924 the federal government began its interstate road assistance program and the State of Kansas began providing improved secondary roads. In 1930 the program was stepped up as a means of providing employment and this was continued and further increased by the Works Progress Administration in 1933.

AVI lost $30,000 in 1925. In 1926 it lost $33,000 and in May, 1927, responded to automobile competition in the classic and unsuccessful manner of present day transit companies: it raised fares and cut service. In applying for the increase Charles Basse, the auditor, observed that a twentieth century marvel other than the automobile was partly responsible. The combine, he said, was also hurting business by reducing the number of itinerant farm hands in harvest season. President Campbell stated that better service could be given as a result of the fare increase, which was from 3¢ to 3.6¢ per mile, making it about a third higher than prevailing steam road fares.

● Here is car 3 at Wichita Station about 1937; the car is standing near the freight station with the Broadview Hotel just to the right. (ES)

As business continued to decline, service was cut as an economy measure. The reduced service was less desirable and resulted in further declines in patronage which were followed by still deeper service cuts. The familiar vicious circle was in full swing. Patronage was never permanently damaged by busses, however. In fact, AVI itself engaged in the bus business.

Through its subsidiary, the Arkansas Valley Transportation Company, the AVI operated a motor coach and truck line over the Meridian Highway, U.S. #81, from Newton to Salina. The service was a substitute for the Salina rail extension, holding the franchise in the event that the extension might someday be built. It also served as a useful and profitable feeder to its parent company. White trucks and "giant" 19-passenger Studebaker busses were featured. The line eventually became The Cardinal Stages but through ticketing and scheduling continued.

There was a time when unregulated operators scraped out an inadequate living running old seven-passenger touring cars at the most heavily traveled hours of the day. They skimmed off enough business to weaken the AVI a little and yet not enough to make a decent living for themselves. When his car wore out, the wildcat operator usually couldn't afford another, so he quit and got another job, but there were always replacements. Like the local jitney drivers, the wildcat driver-owners used to race each other and engage in brawls over passengers. In the middle of the night or in inclement weather the tinhorn operator stayed home while AVI discharged its franchise obligations to his fair weather patrons. The tinhorn needed no franchise. He didn't even need a driver's license. As a usual thing he was completely irresponsible and, in case of accident, not worth suing. John Blood, who was attorney for the AVI, ran for the Kansas State Legislature on a platform of regulation of the tinhorns. He was elected, his bill passed, and that ended the tinhorns. But the AVI had more substantial competition in the form of Greenleaf Stages.

Aaron Greenleaf was no tinhorn. His big Fageol Safety Coaches were the finest intercity busses money could buy. In 1924 he advertised two round trips between Wichita and Hutchinson each day. His schedules were published in the papers and he did a fairly good job of adhering to them. His drivers were reliable. With D. E. Sauder he later founded the mighty Southern Kansas Stage Lines (now the Santa Fe Trailways segment of Continental) but his busses failed to dent the popular AVI. He boasted four one-way runs a day, but AVI had thirty-two.

Other bus and truck lines eventually paralleled the AVI more closely, but they never equalled its service. In 1925 one could come from Hutchinson to Wichita or send a package on three hour's notice via AVI. Today the area has twice the population and is vastly more prosperous, but has no such service. The private automobile put the AVI out of business, but it, nor anything else has thus far replaced it.

THE DEPRESSION: 1929 was a lush year in AVI land. The Valley Center oil field was the center of extensive drilling activity. The Frisco and AVI moved in much valuable oil field material and, before the field became well enough developed to warrant a pipe line, the AVI moved bulk crude oil to the MOP interchange for shipment to the oil refineries in North Wichita. AVI also moved casinghead gasoline which residents along Woodrow in West Riverside considered a menace. Wichita was the air capital, livestock and grain futures were at record high levels and climbing; real estate was booming and newly rich farmers, who had struck oil, were spending money like water. The AVI was losing very little passenger business and freight, both the carload variety and the rapid frequent shipment of foodstuffs and other high value LCL merchandise, was on the increase. The speed with which the interurban could and did move perishables brought it an excellent reputation among shippers of foodstuffs.

1930 was a good year, but the world wide depression finally caught up with the midwest. Airplanes and oil became drugs on the market. A series of very dry years reduced crop yields and pasture at the very time that the market for cereal grains and livestock was declining. The Depression did not strike with the suddenness it exhibited in the east, but when it arrived it was a major economic catastrophe. Only the insurance adjustment business prospered; people began burning down their houses to collect the insurance.

AVI fared only as well as its customers and they did poorly, indeed. In the early Thirties an 18-month old Willys 8 sold for $35.00---three year old Buicks went begging for $75.00---gasoline retailed at 8¢ a gallon and one could buy a Model T Ford in running order for $7.00. With prices like these, only an insurance adjuster could afford to pay 99¢ to ride the AVI from Newton to Wichita, a distance of 27 miles. Even the insurance adjusters' prosperity was short lived; as real estate prices settled down at an unprecedented low level the companies began issuing policies which gave realistically small coverage and discouraged house burning.

Unable to pay its bondholders, the AVI entered receivership in January, 1933, with Warren E. Brown and Charles H. Smyth joint receivers. Subsequently Brown and Robert ("Interurban Bob") Campbell were made trustees in bankruptcy. They were able to keep the road in operation, but maintenance and service slowly declined. Two facts kept creditors from junking the AVI. For one thing, the depressed market for junk made its salvage value very low, and, for another, the line employed nearly a hundred people. With 40% of the employable people of the nation out of work, no one wanted to cut off another payroll and add these AVI people to the army of the unemployed. The creditors included the solvent KG&E, three counties and the Hutchinson Interurban which itself was in precarious financial health.

Let us compare the AVI with another Kansas line which was not so heavily constructed, so luxurious or so highly priced. The Union Traction Company served Coffeyville, with 20,000 population, Independence (13,000) and Parsons, with 16,000 souls. It was 86 miles long. The 59.6 mile AVI served the principal cities of Wichita (111,000), Newton (11,000) and Hutchinson (30,000). The population density is a fairly good indication of the potential business to be found--- yet, in 1935 the UT emerged from receivership as the Union Electric Railway. It had lightweight, one man equipment; main line fares were about 1¢ per mile and the four Independence and five Coffeyville city lines sold three tokens for a dime. Its Independence city system and the main line survived World War II. True, it had corrugated track and home made special work, but people could afford to ride it. The AVI, with its stained glass, luxurious seating and expensive meter cabs (instead of three-for-a-dime streetcars) at the stations, offered a ride of much higher quality but, at 3.6¢ a mile it was priced right out of the market. In the later years the two man AVI crew often outnumbered the passengers.

<u>SOUTHWESTERN INTERURBAN RAILWAY:</u> South of Wichita the little Southwestern Interurban linked Winfield and Arkansas City. A year older than AVI, it had been built by D. H. Siggins of the Siggins Brothers who had constructed the Union Traction Company system in southeastern Kansas. It was much lighter and smaller than the AVI, having only 56 lb. rail and a single substation. Mr. Siggins had personally shoveled ballast and placed ties during its construction and his brother, Owen, was the first motorman.

The line was founded March 24, 1909, to connect Winfield (which had a fine city system) with Arkansas City. The operating forces, as well as the first five cars, came from the Union Traction at Coffeyville. The two double truck interurbans were named Winfield and Arkansas City, appropriately enough. One city car was assigned to the

new city service at Arkansas City while the other two went to help the fleet in Winfield. On June 8th, power was turned on and on June 14th people were invited to ride but the power failed. The following day the still expectant crowd was taken, on the Santa Fe, to the substation at Hackney, where five cars awaited power. At 5:10 PM the motor-generator began turning, but it was another two hours before direct current flowed into the line. The trip proceeded in the pleasant, gathering dusk and when the cars finally reached Arkansas City the fire siren was blown and the town turned out en masse to see the last word in rural transportation.

Despite the enthusiasm of the Siggins Brothers, the line failed to amount to much. Business which in later years consisted mostly of produce was so poor that in 1922 George Theis was able to buy the property for a price variously reported as being from $50,000 to $80,000. As a segment of the AVI empire, which Theis intended, the line would have been valuable, but it was never combined, physically or corporately, with the AVI. On December 30, 1922, the name was changed to "Arkansas City & Winfield Northern Railway Company." The long name apparently was given to compensate for the shortness of the line. It was but fifteen miles in length.

Although the line was rehabilitated and service increased, it was no more successful than the Bethel line had been. It was abandoned on June 8th, 1927.

<u>HUTCHINSON RELOCATION:</u> On July 12, 1929, a flood descended on Hutchinson, washing out the pavement adjacent to the car tracks of the Hutchinson Interurban Railway on Main St. and on Ave. A. The HI could not afford to repair the damage and, after months of waiting, the city took action. HI was formally requested to repair its paving or the city would repeal the jitney ordinance, bringing back competing bus transportation. HI soon thereafter applied to convert any or all of its lines to motor coach operation, and it became apparent that AVI would either have to rebuild several miles of trackage or find another entrance into Hutchinson.

Many influential Hutchinson residents came out in favor of AVI's relocating its entrance. The heavy AVI cars, it must be admitted, were not helping the track, and AVI was running two car freights down Ave. A west of Lorraine St. and onto Main St. in violation of its franchise. Meanwhile, AVI was forced to send its own track crews into Hutchinson to keep the HI track from disintegrating completely.

AVI also tended to favor another entrance into Hutchinson. Passenger business dwindled very rapidly during the early Thirties and, with freight also sagging, AVI sought more sources of revenue. Rock Island freight,

Here is the Wichita newspaper ad which announced the moving of the Hutchinson terminus; about five minutes running time was saved by the change.   (AM)

coming over the main line from Tucumcari and El Paso, when destined for Wichita had to first go through Herrington, the Rock Island junction which was 125 miles farther than via the AVI short cut between Hutchinson and Wichita. AVI now sought to build an extension of its own in Hutchinson to the Rock Island Station. Naturally Wichita cattle and grain men were in favor of this direct route, and many Hutchinson cattle and grain men joined in favoring the proposition as being the lesser of two evils---another plan then suggested would have taken Wichita business to the Rock Island main line via Pratt. Opposing the AVI's plan were those who felt Hutchinson would be better off if AVI were to be eliminated completely (these always felt that AVI tariffs favored Wichita businessmen over those of Hutchinson), the Hutchinson & Northern Railway, and even an undertaker who claimed that AVI's new route would endanger funeral processions.

The Hutchinson & Northern was a little electric switching road owned by Mr. Emerson Carey, the most prominent citizen of Hutchinson. Carey, a man of humble beginnings, made a fortune in Hutchinson, principally in salt; he owned the HI, which at one time had a local system far more extensive than most cities of comparable size could boast. He was likewise a power in politics, being the Junior Senator from Kansas during the Harding administration. Carey had helped AVI enter Hutchinson and in general favored the AVI--- but he also owned the H&N. The H&N served

Above is car 20 of the Southwestern Interurban, one of two Brill Semi-Convertibles built by American, 1909; 41'8" long.

Business was roaringly good when this photo was taken. City car 4 of Southwestern Interurban (American, 1909, 29'5"). (HLH)

several industries in Hutchinson and, by using about a mile of AVI trackage, the Carey salt mine, east of Hutchinson, Carey offered to build a new track to permit the AVI to reach its station. In this way the H&N would have continued to be cut in on the revenues of all loads switched from the AVI to the Rock Island.

Carey obtained permission to build his connecting line from the Hutchinson city commission and, without waiting for ICC approval, began to build the line.

Meanwhile the H1 trackage declined to the point that an interurban split a switch on Avenue A, between Main and Walnut, and crashed into the side of a Birney car operated by one Jesse James. One passenger was injured.

The ICC took about a year to hear all interested parties. The proceedings are full of testimony of people seeking business, employment, or just notice. One communist agitator (who apparently hated Carey) made numerous inflammatory statements in favor of the AVI and probably embarrassed the AVI management.

In early 1932 the ICC granted AVI permission to build its extension. AVI acquired the H&N building materials for which the H&N now had no use and constructed its line, which opened on December 20, 1932. It now operated six round trips daily over the entire line. Passengers for the Golden State Limited could leave Wichita much later because the interurban ran right to the Rock Island station. But the cars no longer terminated across the street from the Santa Fe station, nor did they serve downtown Hutchinson. This was progress; progress away from a true interurban.

THE LEAN YEARS: The Hutchinson relocation failed to save the AVI. At the time it was planned it linked Wichita with its fastest growing trade territory. Southwestern Kansas and the Oklahoma and Texas panhandles had been booming with cattle, oil and natural gas. The Rock Island had built two branches, one of them connecting Liberal with Amarillo, but protracted drought combined with an extended business downturn negated the good effects of this change. The pasture dried up until those cattle which hadn't already died of thirst were starving. Oil sold for 60 cents a barrel and the Hugoton gas field was so vast that there was no ready market for all that gas.

Agriculture was also expanding in the area and the plowed land, unable to produce crops because of lack of rain, began blowing away in the strong winds of the area. This valuable topsoil would then fall, like black snow, on distant points such as Wichita. Farmland sold for less than $1.00 an acre and some was simply abandoned, improvements and all! A vast exodus took place and those who remained had little to sell in Wichita and almost no money. Hence there was very little trade.

The AVI entered this period in good physical condition. It had many recently-overhauled cars and fine track, but classified repairs to the

THE ARKANSAS VALLEY INTERURBAN RAILWAY COMPANY

(ROBERT B. CAMPBELL and WARREN E. BROWN, Trustees.)

R. B. CAMPBELL, Gen. Manager, Wichita, Kan.
CHARLES BASSE, Gen. Auditor and Treasurer, Wichita, Kan.
W. E. STANLEY, General Counsel, "
O. M. MORRISON, Traffic Manager, "
BERNICE V. SHRECK, Secretary, "

A. MARTIN, Superintendent, Wichita, Kan.
ELMER VALLANCE, Master Mechanic, "

Total Mileage, 60.

Pas.	Pas.	Pas.	Pas.	Pas.	Pas.	Mls.	December, 1935	Pas.	Pas.	Pas.	Pas.	Pas.	Pas.
PM	PM	PM	PM	AM	AM	....	LEAVE | ARRIVE	AM	PM	PM	PM	PM	PM
*8 00	*5 40	*3 30	*1245	*1030	*8 00	0	......Wichita......	9 40	12 10	2 28	5 10	7 20	9 40
8 27	6 07	3 57	1 13	10 57	8 27	11.3	...Valley Center...	9 13	11 43	2 01	4 43	6 53	9 13
8 39	6 19	4 09	1 26	11 09	8 39	17.8	.....Sedgwick.....	9 01	11 31	1 49	4 31	6 41	9 01
8 50	6 30	4 20	1 38	11 20	8 50	23.5	arr.Van Arsdale.lve.	8 50	11 20	1 38	4 20	6 30	8 50
9 05	6 45	4 35	1 53	11 35	9 05	29.5	arr....Newton...lve.	*8 30	*1100	*1 20	*4 00	*5 10	*8 30
*8 30	*6 10	*4 00	*1 20	*1100	*8 30	29.5	lve...Newton...arr.	9 05	11 35	1 53	4 35	6 45	9 05
8 50	6 30	4 20	1 38	11 20	8 50	23.5	lve.Van Arsdale.arr.	8 50	11 20	1 38	4 20	6 30	8 50
9 00	6 40	4 30	1 48	11 30	9 00	28.5	.......Halstead......	8 40	11 10	1 25	4 10	6 20	8 40
9 17	6 57	4 47	2 07	11 47	9 17	37.9	.......Burrton......	8 22	10 52	1 07	3 52	6 02	8 22
9 22	7 02	4 52	2 12	11 52	9 22	40.1	......Morrison......	8 17	10 47	1 02	3 47	5 57	8 17
9 45	7 25	5 15	2 40	12 15	9 45	51.6	....Hutchinson....	*7 55	*1025	*1240	*3 25	*5 35	*7 55
PM	PM	PM	PM	PM	AM	.....	ARRIVE | LEAVE	AM	AM	PM	PM	PM	PM

TRACK CONNECTIONS. —At Burrton and Valley Center with the St. Louis-San Francisco. At Hutchinson direct connections with the Rock Island Lines and the Hutchinson & Northern, and through those lines with the Santa Fe and Missouri Pacific. At Wichita with the Midland Valley and Missouri Pacific, also indirect connections with the Santa Fe, Frisco and Rock Island through the Missouri Pacific.

MORRISON, KAN.,
In the Heart of the Burrton Oil Field.

*Daily.   STANDARD—*Central time.*

In the 1936 edition of the "Official Guide," AVI ran this advertisement. Note the prominence given to the oil traffic.

Main Street, Hutchinson, looking north from Avenue A about 1927. AVI cars came in from the right on Avenue A. Photo is from Ray Faubion and Hutchinson Chamber of Commerce. Note one of Hutchinson Interurban's Birneys in the distance.

cars were limited to weekly inspections at which non-durable components such as trolley wheels were replaced, adjustments were made and a minimum of major repairs were carried out. As the years passed and the dust and Depression continued, the cars gradually wore out. It is to the credit of the AVI mechanical and operating forces that disabling road failures did not increase during this period.

The scarlet and cream paint had always clashed with the stained glass windows and restrained, dignified interior decor and now it faded to a sickly pink and ghastly white. Eventually the passenger cars were painted a uniform maroon, without trim.

BALLAST: The weakest link in AVI physical plant was its lack of good track ballast. Except in a few places which had given much trouble, the "ballast" was the natural soil found along the right-of-way. This was sandy loam with some clay. In wet weather it turned to mud and offered a variable and insecure support for the ties, with the result that the track became rapidly misaligned during protracted wet weather. The repeated freezing and thawing of a Kansas winter would cause some misalignment, too.

It was extremely difficult, and at times impossible, to work mud or frozen mud and this meant that there were many days when the track crews could barely accomplish repair, if they could work at all. Also, their services were
CONTINUED ON PAGE 54 -------

A.V.I. OPERATING FIGURES:	1912	1913	1914	1915	1916	1918	1920	1929	1930	1931	1935	1937
Gross Earnings	$136,442	$132,546	$137,454	$140,261	$271,107	$328,611	$547,375	$447,580	$445,469	$306,845	$168,177	$151,983
Operating Expenses	86,702	79,756	79,612	82,150	140,684	228,737	337,254	415,453	401,400	328,946	229,644	238,746
Net Earnings ..	$ 49,740	52,790	57,842	58,111	130,423	99,874	210,121	32,127	44,069	*22,101	*61,467	*86,763
Interest and Taxes	47,965	53,553	58,387	59,691	83,222	95,150	79,646	14,206	21,729	18,066	17,639	17,638
Net Revenue ...	$ 1,775	* $763	* $545	*1,580	$47,201	$4,724	$130,475	$17,921	$22,340	*40,167	*83,158	*106,792

* Loss   As of 1930, AVI's total assets were $3,388,751; however, its working capital was only $42,689.

Continued from Page. 54

Let us take an imaginary trip over the South Emporia line of the Wichita Transportation Corporation in the late spring of 1935, a few weeks before conversion to bus. Our car, a prematurely aged Birney, squeaks and rattles as we proceed eastward on Douglas Avenue and we wonder if it also leaks. The last time we took the streetcar home during a rain storm, people raised their umbrellas inside the car---they needed 'em, too. This car is one of seven, purchased in 1927 and equipped with K-37 controllers and a rear exit door we have never seen used. Sand and deadman equipment have been eliminated to reduce maintenance. Fares have recently been cut to a nickel. Wichita will soon be the second first-class city to convert to 100% motor coach operation.

Our car swings to the right and we are on Emporia Avenue. The motorman throws off and coasts expectantly under a breaker. Our trolley wheel strikes the breaker with a resounding thud and leaves the wire. The motorman is through the door, has replaced the trolley and is back operating the car in no more time than it takes to tell it. "Always lose it on that breaker," he explains. This man knows the line. A few nights later an extra man will come along here at normal speed and bring down the overhead, poles and all, for several hundred feet. "I lost a trolley there but good last week," says the motorman. "The base tore right off the roof and the whole thing fell onto the street."

As we enter the Lincoln St. switch our car veers to the left and goes up the wrong track. "Spring broke some time ago," explains the motorman. "They gave us a little sponge rubber plug to replace it but it does not work right. There's too much danger of going on the ground there, so, if we don't have a meet, we all use this side."

As we get farther south, beyond the Santa Fe tracks, the lights become noticeably dimmer. Sparks fly along the broken bonds at the low joints behind. We can remember, two short years ago, when we came down here in nothing flat; there were more passenger stops, but the lights then burned brightly. Now the track is broken in so many places that the power can not flow through it and must go by way of devious water pipes. We reflect that as much power is being wasted getting to the car as is being consumed, and mention this to the motorman when he wyes at Harry St. "Could be," he replies; "Watch this." With the brake set, he flips the controller handle around onto the brass. The lights virtually go out. Fireworks flare momentarily along the track ahead at the ruined joints. The circuit breaker stays closed. The trolley fuse does not blow. He releases the air. With a whistling snort the compressor starts thumping, torpidly. The car groans to a sluggish start. In two blocks of parallel running we reach normal series speed at which speed the violently oscillating car throws its trolley. We replace it for the tired man who grimly feeds up again. "This must be the worst track in town," we venture. He eyes us grimly: "Well, it's all so bad it is hard to say. There are several feet in the first block on North Main where the head is broken clean off the rail. We go through there on the flanges and pray."

Conditions in other midwestern cities were similar. After abandonment at Enid, Oklahoma, the first day of dismantling the system produced a casualty. One of the men climbed a pole to remove a span wire; the pole broke off at the ground under his weight. The Hutchinson Interurban was in especially bad physical condition.

<u>ABANDONMENT OF PASSENGER SERVICE:</u> AVI at length gave up trying to attract passenger business and in the summer of 1938 applied for permission to abandon all passenger runs. Permission was received and on July 31, 1938, the last passenger car pulled in and the line became freight only. Only six men lost their jobs, so slight had passenger business become.

Tom H. Newman, the oldest trainman on the line had this to say: "I have travel-

'Twas a gloomy day as car 12 made its way north out of Wichita back in 1938, and equally gloomy was the plight of AVI's passenger business. On July 31, 1938, AVI became a freight-only line, ending the dream of George Theis forever. (ES)

ed a million and a half miles on the Hutchinson to Wichita route, both as a passenger and freight motorman. I started July 6, 1911, when the company only had one car. I've made 13,855 round trips. There were days when the AVI traffic was so important that a telegraphed message from a wayside station between Wichita and Hutchinson saying the train was late would hold a Santa Fe train in Hutchinson until it arrived with a load of 'transfers.' I've picked up more than a hundred passengers on Main St. in Hutchinson many times on week days. I think it's partly our own fault we lost out. In the old days rates were so high that when autos began to come people bought them to save money. Now rates are low, but people are so used to autos they don't want to ride interurbans. Another thing that wasn't good for us was putting on limited cars. In the old days every car stopped everywhere, even if there was only one passenger. We weren't in such a big hurry, but we kept going every hour and twenty minutes all day. I told the president I thought we were making a big mistake when the limiteds went on. Farm people were our biggest business and they couldn't keep track of which car was which. They'd come down to the depot and when the limiteds went through they'd be mad. You couldn't blame them---I'd have felt like throwing rocks at the car, too. So they all bought autos."

One of the Wichita newspapers overdid the passenger abandonment story, reporting complete abandonment. It came back the next day with an elaborate discussion of the fact that the company could now devote all its energies and resources to freight without having passenger service interfere, but the brave effort to make passenger abandonment palatable had a hollow sound. True, the passenger business had gone down the drain and there was no use crawling in after it--- but the fact remained that an interurban had become a short line railroad from desperate necessity rather than from choice.

A copy of this editorial has been saved and is reprinted in the adjoining column. Readers may judge for themselves whether or not its sentiments were valid.

The A. V. I. Finds Its Niche

MORE than a quarter century ago there blossomed on the American scene scores of interurban lines, most of them short systems connecting a small group of cities and financed by local capital. But the future looked bright for these new electric lines. Prophets predicted they would eventually become the backbone of the nation's transportation system.

Time has proved that prediction false. The steam lines had some influence on the interurban passenger train but the automobile had more. Short haul passengers could make the trip to town or to neighboring communities more conveniently in their own cars.

But the interurban lines did not pass into the discard. Instead what at first was considered a minor field of activity has become their major source of business—freight. Such a line is the Arkansas Valley Interurban Railway Company, which now proposes to abandon completely its passenger service and greatly enlarge its freight facilities and service.

The A. V. I., which has been an operating transportation unit for 27 years, travels thru one of the richest agricultural territories in all of Kansas. Starting at Wichita, the line travels northwest, connecting with large and small communities and providing an important addition to the freight transportation facilities of this city.

The A. V. I., in the quarter century of its busy lifetime, has contributed millions of dollars in business to Wichita. It is good news to learn that, under the able management of Robert B. Campbell, the road will expand its freight service and play a still greater part in the Wichita of the future.

The attractive Wichita Station of AVI felt the tread of its last passenger on July 31, 1938. The building eventually became a radio studio.

Men of the AVI, although in quite different categories, were Motorman Art Spalding at the controls of car 12 and President George Theis, Jr. whose untimely death was a hard blow. (ES) (MGT)

MEN OF A.V.I.: The AVI was a pleasant, if not highly paid, place to work. Art Spaulding, president of the Amalgamated trainmen's union, said, "They were nice people to deal with. We did not have much trouble settling our few grievances. We had one standing complaint. The pay was substandard." Spaulding's union represented the trainmen under an open shop contract. Other employees were unorganized. The company never had a strike.

The AVI was not a spit-and-polish line. The cars and stations were kept presentably clean, but neatness was not a fetish, especially in the shops. The atmosphere was generally relaxed and friendly. The line was small enough to prevent intense specialization. An AVI shop man could become quite versatile and in so doing reduced the chance of boredom.

Boredom was more of a problem in the substations. You attend the machinery for sixteen hours a day and sleep the other eight in an apartment above the dynamo room. An occasional car goes by. You hope the KG&E will need a switch thrown so that you can pick up a little extra pay, and you need that extra pay. In 1934 all three subs cost a total of $3,768.40 for 17,520 hours of direct labor. This did not include the free rent, utilities and garden plots provided. No inspector makes you scrub the floor and polish the brass and you can work in the garden while on duty, but it's a dull

life. Only the Burrton sub was in town. The other two didn't even have neighbors. In the beginning, substation men had one day off a month but they complained until they got two days monthly, according to Elmer Vallance.

Way & Structures was an important, outdoor job. You gauged the track that steered the car, you built the trestles which supported it, and when the crest of a flood deposited an overload of debris on the trestle you might even risk your life to clear it. Other men made plans and raised money---but YOU BUILT THE RAILROAD.

AVI trainmen had a pleasant, adventurous life. People to meet, schedules to keep, blizzards to buck, floods to ford and summer heat that called forth a motorman's best power-saving techniques to keep the motors cool. There was no one man operation except perhaps at Bethel. The job was challenging, but one could handle it and still enjoy life. It was glamorous, too; trainmen were looked up to by much of the public---especially by girls and small children.

President George Theis was typical of top management who planned and financed the AVI. As a young man he left his farm home and found employment which became so remunerative that he was able to send his parents enough money to hire a man to take his place on the farm, pay his board and room and, eventually, to start a bank. While more

mature men struggled to make a living, Theis by a fortunate combination of industry and talent became not only wealthy but a valued member of the community as well. When crop failures threatened to send his farmer clients back to Illinois he made numerous personal loans to men he knew to be capable farmers, thus enabling them to stay on their land another year. The men were not good enough risks to be given credit by his bank yet his personal loans drew no interest. His great sense of civic responsibility was, perhaps, the reason he lavished so much money and effort on the unremunerative AVI. He was popular. We have interviewed former AVI people from all levels of the organization and have yet to hear one derogatory thing said of him. These people regard him as having been highly competent to manage AVI affairs. Time and again we have heard one of them say, "Now, if George Theis had only lived- - - -". But he didn't. In July of 1927 he was killed in an airplance ground accident at an air show at Travel Air Field. Had his plans to build and buy north to Salina materialized, the line would almost certainly be running today (although not necessarily with passenger service and with electric power). The AVI's most hopeful years were clearly those when he controlled it. During this time he held from 81% to 51% of the common stock, stock which controlled the company but which never at any time paid dividends. His will provided a bequest of $1,000 to each official and $277.50 to each other employee with three

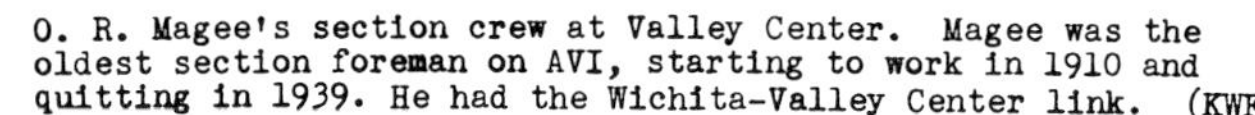

Here "Interurban Bob" Campbell (right) stands with a fellow officer in front of trailer 102 preparatory to an excursion trip to drum up freight business. (AM)

O. R. Magee's section crew at Valley Center. Magee was the oldest section foreman on AVI, starting to work in 1910 and quitting in 1939. He had the Wichita-Valley Center link. (KWF)

or more years seniority at the time of his death.

His successor, as president, was Robert B. (Interurban Bob) Campbell, who had been General Manager prior to Theis' death. Mr. Campbell had also served as general manager of the Wichita Transportation Corporation which succeeded Wichita Railway & Light Company and, as a boy, had had the dubious distinction of masterminding certain disruptions in the local mule car service. The cars were single truck affairs with doors which locked from the outside. A group of boys would board the rear platform of a car and begin rocking it. Soon the driver would start back through the car to rid himself of the undesirable deadheads. Upon reaching the rear door he'd find it locked from the outside and would turn to find another boy locking the front door, also from the outside. The boys, on the two open platforms, would then drive the mule anywhere on the system that fancy might dictate, or until they met another car. Bob's father used to disclaim, at the supper table on what he would do to "those awful boys" when and if he should catch them---and young Bob listened piously at his side. Such was Mr. Campbell's early preparation for a career in transit.

We do not know the exact number of AVI's employees, but it is estimated that before the first World War the monthly payroll ranged from $15,000 to $20,000. The 60-mile line was divided into seven sections, each with its own section crew, comprising a foreman and from six to ten men, probably giving a total of about seventy men in that department. The trainmen totalled about 25 motormen, 25 conductors, six brakemen and about 15 shop workers. The three dispatchers had their headquarters in the Wichita Station. Each of the seven ticket-selling stations of the line had an agent working one shift, while Wichita, Hutchinson and Newton had two agents working two shifts. In the general offices at Wichita there were approximately fifteen people, so we have a grand total of about 170 employees when AVI was at its peak.

AVI section hands drew as little as 25¢ per hour in the early Thirties and station agents got but $73.00 per month. Section foremen fared somewhat better, receiving up to $110 monthly. There was no pension plan until the Railroad Retirement Act of 1935 came into being.

Only the trainmen were unionized, belonging to the Amalgamated Association of Street & Electric Railroad Employees of America.

AVI employees had permanent passes in the form of green cards. The company also exchanged pass privileges with the steam lines, but an AVI employee wishing to take a steam road trip had to apply in advance for a special one-time pass which was collected by the steam road conductor.

<u>JOHN R. COX:</u> Abandonment of passenger service did not solve AVI's dilemma. On March 25, 1939, AVI's preferred creditors closed in and the road was offered for sale. The minimum bid acceptable to Judge Richard J. Hopkins, of the U.S. District Court, was $75,000 plus $104,186 in back taxes owed to Reno, Harvey and Sedgwick Counties. Claude I. Depew, attorney for AVI, received no bids and announced that he would file a motion in Federal Court to sell the property piecemeal. This would be done immediately unless someone would make a private bid which would be subject to Court approval. Superintendent Ailee Martin issued a bulletin urging all employees to discharge their duties faithfully and advising them that while the situation was grave, all was not necessarily lost. Sure enough, at the last minute a private bidder, in the person of John R. Cox of Chicago, appeared.

After much negotiation Cox arranged with the commissioners of the three counties to compromise back taxes at the rate of $100 per year for the years 1932 through 1937, one year's taxes being cancelled for each year of successful operation of the line.

He would pay 1938 and 1939 taxes in full, and pay all future taxes. As the counties had only a second lien on the road and, as its junk value would have exceeded the prior lien of $75,000 by only about $25,000, and as the AVI provided a $300,000 annual payroll to about 85 people, the counties agreed. By July 20 an agreement had been put in writing but not yet signed. On July 21, State Senator Walter F. Jones, representing the Hutchinson City Commission, protested the tax deal. "The city has no part in this compromise which is being undertaken by the County Commissioners but it is money of the taxpayers of Hutchinson that is proposed to be compromised away. It is a promotion scheme to benefit others and the taxpayers of Hutchinson have a right to object," cried Jones. Others objected on the grounds that AVI no longer was a passenger line and its freight trains were a liability rather than an asset to beautiful city streets. AVI was not without its defenders.

Cox assured the press that he was not a front man for a steam railroad and that he was negotiating for a hundred thousand ties and two carloads of bridge timbers. He also stated that he planned to make his home in Wichita and personally operate the AVI. Finally, on September 1, 1939, Cox signed agreements with the various county commissioners and returned to Chicago to raise the money. This he failed to do.

The Arkansas Valley Railway

Motive power of the Arkansas Valley Railway consisted of three units: two 44-ton, 380 HP diesel-electric locomotives (92 & 93) and a Brill gas-electric car (91). Here #92 is seen at Newton in 1942, ready to leave for Van Arsdale and Hutchinson on the noon freight. (ES)

<u>ARKANSAS VALLEY RAILWAY:</u> Cox had done one thing. He had, at last, paved the way for the sale of the line and, in November 1939, the H. E. Salzburg Company, without fanfare, purchased the AVI. They promptly changed its name to THE ARKANSAS VALLEY RAILWAY, INC. and ordered two diesel locomotives. The change from interurban to short line railway was complete. Mr. M. H. Snerson, a Salzburg man, was named General Manager. Snerson had other properties to manage and left Assistant General Manager Welcher in charge at Wichita. E. R. Vallance became the new Superintendent.

Elmer Robinson Vallance was one of the original AVI men and in March 1941 succeeded Welcher as Assistant General Manager. The man who prepared the first AVI cars for service thus was the operating head of the road at the time of its abandonment.

The Salzburg firm was a combined scrap and operating company. It purchased sickly interurban lines and operated them as long as they held together and could be made to pay....then they dismantled them. They had six years to operate the AVR before they would be able to scrap it without paying back taxes and after the first year they prepared for indefinite operation, buying two 44-ton G.E. diesel electrics and a second-hand Brill gas-electric car.

<u>DIESELIZATION & ABANDONMENT:</u> On Sunday, October 20, 1940, three passenger cars (4, 5, 8) came out of retirement to make a final passenger run bringing Newton and Hutchinson business and civic leaders to Wichita, where they boarded rented Frisco coaches

In these three photos by Eugene Sabin we see:

Above, 91 hauling a long train; AVI burned out its motors once hauling too many cars.

Left, Cars 4 and 8 were resurrected to run one last time celebrating dieselization of the AVR. They brought shippers to Wichita on October 20, 1940 who were returned in Frisco cars hauled by AVR 93, seen below leaving the Wichita Station.

and were pulled back by a diesel. The purpose of the trip was to sell the freight service. Complete dieselization followed, and trolley wire and substations were removed (except for the mile of joint H&N trackage in Hutchinson). The dieselized AVR succeeded in making ends meet, but little more.

The Neutrality Act was repealed. Business in Wichita's aircraft plants boomed but AVR did not serve a single defense plant. Japan gave the United States a premature and unwanted Christmas present in 1941. Immediately there arose a scrap metal shortage, made more acute by the fact that the price of scrap had been set by the government at such a low figure that the usual suppliers, shorn of their cheap help by the war boom, could no longer supply it. The government eyed the AVR rails, which could be easily salvaged, hungrily.

Costs of operation soared. The road could be junked and made to pay off in that way and no one knew it better than the Salzburg management. Abandonment brought no outcry about throwing people out of work. AVR men who, a few years before, had been "too old to hire" when so many "bright, young men are available," had suddenly become "mature, responsible employees" who were draft exempt.

In May 1942 part of the Seneca St. trestle in Wichita washed out; it was the type of thing which could have been repaired in a week, but it gave one more reason for abandonment. So in that month Salzburg asked the Interstate Commerce Commission for permission to abandon the whole line. Boeing's Wichita Division and the Office of Defense Transportation considered the possibility of acquiring the AVR and relocating it so as to serve the three aircraft plants south and east of Wichita but nothing came of it.

There was now no one to oppose abandonment except Howard Carey and his Hutchinson & Northern. The ICC authorized the abandonment provided that any part of the line be sold to any bidder desiring to continue the rail operation; Carey wanted that segment from Burrton to Hutchinson to give Hutchinson neutral connections with the Frisco.

However, the government requisitioned the railway through the War Production Board for scrap and operation ceased on the evening of July 23, 1942. The last train reached Wichita the following day. The Salzburg Company dismantled the line as far as the Carey mine where the H&N trackage rights began; this mile of AVR trackage Carey saved and it is operating today, a still useful remnant of an enterprise which promised much and which

would have fulfilled that promise had not the automobile and the paved rural road superceded it.

Fourteen years have scattered the AVI men across the face of the continent. Some are in retirement, many have much better jobs, but the AVI lives on in their memories almost as vividly as if #8 were just leaving Burrton with a baggage compartment full of raw milk for the DeCoursey processing plant at Wichita. Without the helpful interest of these men this account could never have been written.

The AVI Ladies' Auxiliary today meets regularly. Former AVI men on the remote Pacific Coast still keep in touch with each other. Allison Chandler closes his excellent account of the AVI, "Trolley Through The Countryside," with this comment from Mr. D. D. Peachy of Hutchinson: "I've been away from the AVI for a little over twenty years, but I don't believe there is a month which passes that I don't dream that the officials of the road have decided to try to operate it again and I have gone back to work for them."

Today, fourteen years afterwards, there remain tangible evidences of AVI. On the campus of Bethel College in Newton, four passenger car bodies (2, 9, 102 and another) are neatly arranged in horseshoe design to provide living quarters for students; two AVI reefer bodies nearby are fashioned into the campus repair shop. AVI 10 is on U.S. Highway 50 South 16 miles northeast of Newton as a diner. Three AVI passenger car bodies are near Broadway and 53rd St. in Wichita Heights in use as living quarters. At least two others are in use on farms in the area as storage sheds. Locomotive 602 is still running on the North Shore.

The beautiful Wichita Station is in use today as the headquarters of the KAKE Broadcasting Company. The Valley Center substation is now an apartment building, but the Van Arsdale sub is abandoned and in bad shape. The Burrton sub is vacant but the living quarters are in use. The grade and abutments of the Santa Fe overpass are in evidence, and the Newton police use the southern slope for their pistol range. At Hutchinson, the AVI Station houses Greyhound and Continental Trailways busses and the Newton Station has been torn down.

A bit of AVI's rail system still lives; six days a week the H&N's little electric locomotives may be seen running along the mile of ex-AVI rails linking the Carey salt mine with that company's evaporative plant.

TERMINAL AND SHOP PLANS

OF THE

ARKANSAS VALLEY INTERURBAN RY. CO.

As of April 21, 1921   *Data: The Electrical Inspection Bureau*

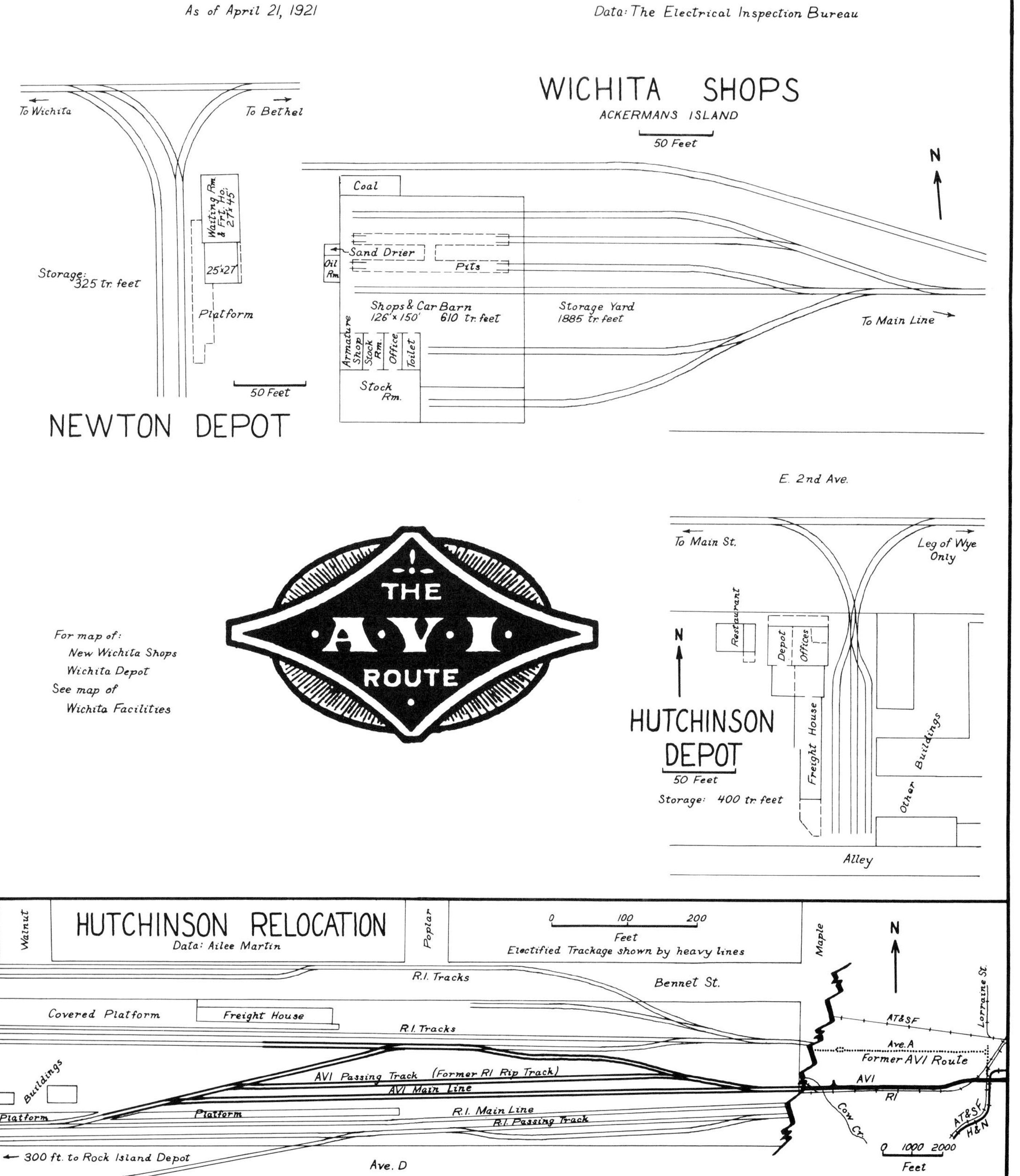

Chapter 3

Facilities

<u>STATIONS:</u> AVI's first Wichita depot was in the Beacon Building with a small wood & stucco freight station on the northeast corner of First & Water Sts. This was on the northwest fringe of the downtown district, easily accessible by streetcar from all parts of the city. This was built and operated as a "temporary" depot, with wide circulation being given to AVI's announced intention of constructing a more commodious station as soon as traffic demanded.

The upsurge in traffic was not long in making itself felt, and Wichita got a more fitting AVI terminal building soon after the line opened. This second depot building was of brick construction, was two stories high, and was built on the same site as the first station. Cars backed into First St. from Main and into the station yard. Leaving the station yard they headed out into First St., ran half a block east to Main and then north on Main and out of town. AVI's offices were located in this building, as were a waiting room, lost & found, ticket office, etc. The building cost $48,000. Around the corner on Water St. AVI built a two-track shop building which had one of the most inconvenient track arrangements imaginable (see map, page 28).

By 1921, this second depot had outlived its usefulness and was retired in favor of one of the most attractive interurban depots ever constructed in the southwest. Located on the north side of Douglas Ave. just east of the Arkansas River, this third depot was also of brick construction and was also two stories in height. It contained a spacious high-ceilinged waiting room, a large ticket office and baggage room in the north part of the building, and a foyer to the street lined with a succession of small retail shops. Upstairs were AVI's general offices. Cars loaded at the rear of the station, on a loop which they negotiated in a counter-clockwise direction. A steel & concrete train shed protected passengers as they boarded the cars. Within the loop were two stub tracks to permit extra cars to be held available as needed. About two hundred feet from the back of the station was a second AVI brick building, the freight house; on its two stub tracks loaded the express cars and trailers, and upstairs was the trainmen's room. Coincidentally with the opening of this station, AVI cars ceased using the local street railway's tracks; AVI's track from 21st & Market to Mascot St., approximately three-quarters of a mile, was abandoned. In its place, a new route was built completely on private right of way, nearly two miles of which was within scenic Sim Park. This new line ran across Ackerman's Island, where AVI constructed new shops at this time.

The Newton depot was originally in a brick office building on East Fifth St. adjacent to

AVI's third and last station in Wichita was this handsome structure. Facing on Douglas Ave. at the river, it measured 100 x 100 feet and was built of dark red tapestry brick with stone trimmings and green tile roof. AVI's offices were upstairs. At the rear was a loop, on which car 2 was standing when this photo was taken. Streetcar tracks ran in foreground.

the Santa Fe Station (which was on the corner of Main & Fifth). Later AVI moved its Newton headquarters a block west on Fifth St. into a modest one-story brick building containing a waiting room, ticket office, baggage room and freight headquarters. A small yard alongside the depot provided two or three tracks for switching and wyeing purposes; this yard was quite deep, running almost all the way back to the Santa Fe tracks.

In Hutchinson, AVI had its second largest station, located on E. Second Ave., between Walnut and Poplar Sts. This was a two story brick building with a three-track yard along the east side of the station building. AVI's freight and baggage business was accommodated by a freight platform running alongside the

building. Passengers alighted on a concrete platform running into the yard about fifty feet from the sidewalk; cars backed into the yard prior to discharging their passengers.

Burrton certainly had an elaborate depot for a town its size. The building was an early functional type, utilizing glass walls and simple architectural lines. It was a multi-purpose structure: the passenger depot was at the west end; the west wall was completely of glass and afforded an excellent view not only of the AVI's main line, but the Frisco's Ellsworth branch and the Santa Fe's

INTERURBANS

1: The Burrton Station---combining waiting room, substation, and freight room in one glass building.

2: Waiting room, Wichita Station.

3: Interior of Ackerman's Island Shops, 1923.

4: Waco Ave. front of Wichita freight house, 1923.

5: Six-track shop on Ackerman's Island, Wichita. This was the building moved piecemeal by WPA.

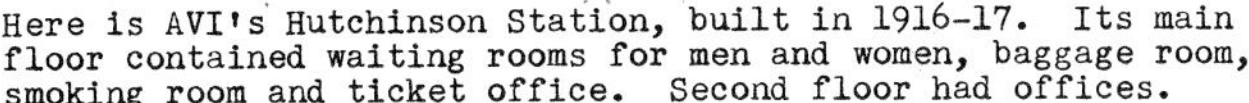

Here is AVI's Hutchinson Station, built in 1916-17. Its main floor contained waiting rooms for men and women, baggage room, smoking room and ticket office. Second floor had offices.

AVI's second Newton Station was this modest structure. Also of brick construction, this building provided the usual facilities for passengers, baggage and freight.

main line with numerous fast trains. In the central portion of this building was a substation, housing two motor-generator sets and their related switch gear; in an unusual departure from the usual practise, transformers were placed outside the sub building. The freight and baggage room occupied the eastern portion of this building. Adjoining this building was a residence for the substation attendant, also of brick but of more conventional architecture.

At Van Arsdale, a small frame shelter, open on one side, afforded waiting facilities for passengers. Van Arsdale was not a town, hence had a modest facility. It did have a brick substation, however.

Halstead had a brick station, one story high and uninspired architecturally. It had an agent on duty, and the usual waiting room and baggage and express facilities.

Valley Center and Sedgwick had one story frame depots of the usual type; both had agents on duty, and both had sidings.

The shelter houses scattered all along the line at section lines and road crossings were modest wooden structures possibly eight feet square with a peaked roof; each contained four back-to-back V-shaped benches for the convenience of passengers.

OVERHEAD AND FEEDER: The AVI made small use of overhead special work. At a siding there would be two parallel, charged, trolley wires. The conductor, in addition to throwing the switch, would move the trolley from one wire to the other. The company also used double trolley wire at various points on the system. Each trolley wire was size 4/0 and there was a 4/0 feeder the entire length of the line. The double trolley wire served as an auxilliary feeder but did not seem to be installed for that reason. In later years the AVI used an additional 4/0 feeder from Burrton substation to the circuit breaker near Brandy Lake and installed a 500 MCM equivalent aluminum feeder from Wichita plant of the Kansas Gas & Electric to 29th St., north of Wichita.

POWER SUPPLY: Direct current as far north as 29th St. in Wichita came from the Kansas Gas & Electric, which had four motor-generator sets in its new Wichita plant, built at the same time that the AVI was being built. Motors were General Electric type ATI, 720 HP, 2300 volt. Generators were GE type MPC, 910 amperes, 550 volts DC.

In later years the voltage from Wichita plant was 600. We have no positive information concerning the voltage when the line was built. The customary voltage of that time was 550 to the line. North of 29th St. the voltage was always 600. The AVI had its own substations: Valley Center, Van Arsdale and Burrton. KG&E supplied 60,000 volt, 3-phase power to the substations.

Equipment in the substations consisted of:

Station	M-G Sets	Transformers
Valley Center	1 200 KVA & 1 300 KVA Allis-Chalmers	3 150 KVA 60,000/2300V - General Electric
Van Arsdale	2 300 KVA Allis-Chalmers	3 150 KVA 60,000/2400V - G.E.
Burrton	2 300 KVA Gen. Electric	3 150 KVA 60,000/2100V- G.E.

The equipment at Valley Center cost $7,000. At Van Arsdale it totalled $7,500 and at Burrton, $7,600.

Valley Center and Van Arsdale were built of unglazed brick with a large two-story transformer vault at the rear and an attendant's quarters above the dynamo room. The buildings were constructed in 1911 and cost $4,000 each. The Burrton transformers were located in the open and the two MG sets were in a small room in the combined passenger, freight and substation. This building cost $3,000. The attendant's cottage was a separate building. These buildings were of long-lasting tapestry brick and much glass was used in their design. The Burrton substation was built in 1915.

When the Hutchinson extension was built the KG&E extended its 60,000 volt transmission line to Burrton and again the interurban and the power company shared a right-of-way. Beyond Burrton the Kansas Power & Light Co. built an intertie to the KG&E line, again on a joint right-of-way with the AVI. Thus AVI was able to use power company poles for its trolley wire over almost its entire length.

At Hutchinson, the AVI obtained power from the Hutchinson Interurban which, name notwithstanding, oiperated the city system in that city. The exact source of this power, from 1915 until the building of the Carey salt plant in 1918, is in doubt. There was, apparently, a steam-generating electric plant at Hutchinson for the city system but we can learn no details.

After the new Carey salt plant was opened, in 1918, it generated 600v D.C. for itself, the city system, the AVI and, apparently, the elevator at the mine (which opened in 1922). The plant had two direct-connected 1250 KVA 2300v generators with reciprocating steam engines. These were apparently A.C., although the bulk of the power requirements at the beginning of operation were D.C. In later years KP&L provided power with a 600 volt, 300 KW rotary-converter. The mine elevator and the entire plant now (1977) run on purchased A.C. and the 42-gauge mine railroad uses 250-volt D.C. from a solid state converter; it formerly used a rotary-converter.

(continued on P. 55)

SHOPS: AVI's car maintenance in the early days was done at a small shop located on Water St. around the corner from First St. It was cramped, having but two tracks. In 1921, coincident with the new line into Wichita, the new Wichita Depot, and the discontinuance of using streetcar tracks to enter that city, AVI built a new concrete block shop building on the north end of Ackerman's Island. The new shop contained six tracks, was well equipped, and might have been in use until abandonment had it not been for the city's decision to remove the island bodily.

The stock market crashed in 1929; the nation entered a prolonged business depression; a new administration came into power in Washington; one of its major acts was the creation of the WPA---the Works Progress Administration. The most serious product of the depression was unemployment; the WPA was established to construct public works with a maximum use of direct labor and a minimum use of materials. The use of power machinery, even animal power, was virtually forbidden. While gigantic and highly efficient earth moving and concrete mixing machinery stood idle, men with shovels and mortar boxes moved mountains and poured paving much as it is done in the Orient. When one sees a thirty foot long bridge today with the inscription, "WPA, 1935-1936-1937," it doesn't mean that the bridge washed out repeatedly; it simply means that it took that long to build it the hard way. Obviously the public works program was distinctly secondary to the end of providing employment. If one who has not witnessed the great depression thinks this fantastic, we can only say that at that time most Americans favored the program and that the depression itself was fantastic.

One such WPA project was the removal of Ackerman's Island in Wichita. The island lay in the Big Arkansas River between the mouth of the Little Arkansas River and Douglas Avenue. AVI's shops were located at the northern end and a large ball park (a source of intermittent revenue for AVI) occupied the center. The south end of the island was crossed by the AVI, the MOP, and at the extreme southern end the island was touched by the trestle of the Wichita Transportation Corporation whose University, Mt. Carmel and Orient Shops streetcars could not use the Douglas Ave. bridge for fear of scaring horses! As downtown Wichita real estate became more valuable, some owners had added increments to their land by filling in the eastern river flood plain and thus pushing the bank closer to Ackerman's Island. As the channel narrowed, it became a serious flood threat (such a narrowed river has, in fact, flooded Kansas City with devastating effects). With such important structures as the Broadview Hotel and the AVI Station on reclaimed land, it was obviously impractical to dig out the original flood plain. The alternative was to remove the half mile long island and this was done by the WPA, a wheelbarrow

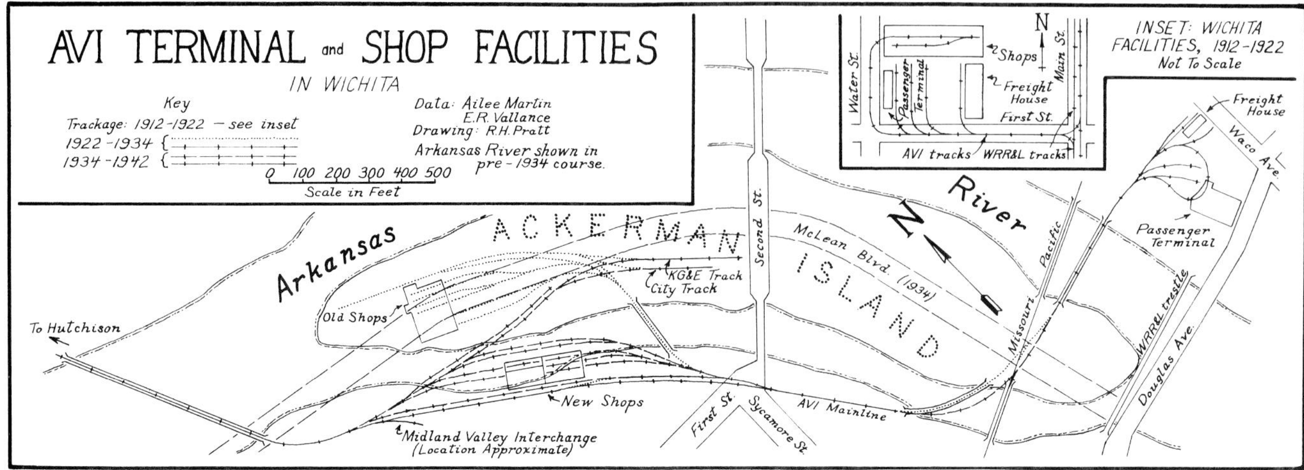

Here we show the old and new passenger and freight facilities of AVI in Wichita. In the inset is the old setup at First & Water Sts., while the Ackerman Island Shops and the WPA-built shops are shown in large map, along with the new passenger and freight facilities on Douglas and Waco Avenues. (Dick Pratt Map)

full at a time, with human horsepower. The WTC tore out its trestle and its two remaining car lines, University and Orient Shops, were, with Cleveland and Pattie Ave. east of the river, converted to busses--- which operated over the Douglas Avenue Bridge, there being few horses remaining to scare. In the process of removing the island, AVI received new shops, free.

The WPA-built shops were located on the west bank of the river about a mile northwest of AVI's station. The concrete pits and floor were mixed by hand, the blocks were carried up the scaffold by hand, the roof rafters were sawed by hand. Usable material from the old shops was brought over, reportedly in wheelbarrows---a 600 foot journey. Thus AVI gained the distinction of having hand-made shops. The entire project was done by the WPA at public expense; it cost AVI nothing. All of AVI's maintenance and repair work was done in Wichita; outlying cities and towns had no facilities to do any of this work.

<u>BRIDGES:</u> AVI's concrete viaducts brought it fame. Not only were these structures sturdy and long lived, but had an aesthetic grace which made them a joy to behold. Even today, years after abandonment, some of the viaducts still stand, a mute monument to the dead interurban.

'Twas not ever thus, however. When it first built its system, AVI followed the customary practise of crossing streams by means of pile trestles. Even as late as 1922 AVI built pile trestles---five were constructed on the line relocation in Wichita; these were the only major timber trestles on the line at that time and were a source of trouble in later years. WPA filled in two of these trestles when it re-

moved Ackerman's Island.

While AVI's route presented comparatively level topography, AVI was forced to bridge several rivers and creeks. The Big Arkansas River in west central Wichita was crossed twice between Central and Douglas Avenues by an AVI track curving in from the northwest, both crossings being on wood pile bridges. The Little Arkansas was crossed by the electric interurban line at 21st St. in northwest Wichita, also on a wood pile bridge. Between Wichita and Valley Center a small creek required a concrete bridge, and in some strange manner repeated rains so weakened the creek bed that it gave way and the bridge sank out of sight; a wood pile bridge was the answer to this unruly problem. A concrete bridge was used to cross Jester Creek between Valley Center and Sedgwick. At Sedgwick, Sand Creek was crossed by a wood pile bridge,

For 27 years electric trains sped over, steam trains thundered under; here is the overpass on the Newton branch near Van Arsdale. Today the abutments remain, and Santa Fe's Super Chief, El Capitan and Chief do some of their fastest running on the Newton-Hutchinson stretch of main line.

In this photo, a car of the 3-10 Class is seen heading toward Wichita.

while a concrete structure supported AVI tracks over Emma Creek just west of Van Arsdale. Sand Creek in West Newton needed a wood pile bridge, on the Bethel line it had a concrete structure which accommodated vehicular traffic as well. At Halstead, a concrete viaduct took the interurban over the Little Arkansas River. In Hutchinson AVI skirted the edge of unpredictable Cow Creek, but no crossing was necessary.

Only one grade separation was built: that which carried AVI rails 26 higher than the Santa Fe main line; this overpass was a mile northeast of Van Arsdale. It was constructed in 1911 when the line to Newton was built; at that time freight occupied a minor place in AVI's plans and no effort was made to ease the grade of approaches. In later years, the abrupt climb to this overpass was to limit the tonnage ratings of all AVI freight power.

AVI's freight & office building, First & Water Sts., Wichita.

Typical concrete bridge with car 2 crossing it, about 1916.

Chapter 4

Cars

AVI's cars were, with the exception of 3-10, a heterogeneous lot. Some were big, but most were small. Some were attractive and some were downright ugly. In size they ranged from a 50-ton steel locomotive down to a smaller-than-standard Birney. None of them could work together in multiple unit; AVI's trains consisted of a single motor car dragging whatever happened to be coupled on behind---and mixed passenger and freight trains were known. All ran on 600 volts DC, or as near an approximation of same as the somewhat fragile (in later years) system of substations could deliver.

PASSENGER CARS: This category was headed by car 12, a 56' steel combo built new by American at the time the Hutchinson extension was opened. Next, AVI seemed to rate car 2, a long composite combo purchased used from the Michigan United. Then came cars 3-10, a batch of St. Louis composite combos somewhat smaller than were usually encountered on interurban lines. There seems never to have been a 13, and car 14 was soon demotorized and renumbered 101. Minor passenger motors were 1, First 2, 11 and 15. Two city cars, 51 and 100, completed the roster of motor cars. Two passenger trailers, 101 and 102, appeared about 1921.

Passenger cars originally were painted dark green with gold trim. In 1928, President Bob Campbell decided that in order to reduce accidents, cars would be painted in "one of the loudest color schemes I could lay my hands on." This turned out to be a flaming red below the belt line, and ivory above. In 1935, probably as an economy move, passenger cars were repainted a solid maroon. Air horns on passenger cars were a single horn, as compared to a double horn on express motors and a triple tone on the locomotives.

EXPRESS & WORK CARS: Heading this category was the 203, a steel express motor built by American in 1916. A composite counterpart, the 202, was built a year earlier. These motors, carrying freight on board, also hauled sizeable trains. An earlier composite express motor, the 201, was converted into AVI's line car. Flatbed work motor 301 doubled as a line car in construction years, but was rebuilt into 601.

LOCOMOTIVES: AVI had but two locomotives, 601 and 602. 601 was a home-built job, while 602 was a standard GE steel steeple cab. Both were used in extra service as AVI's freight business could be hauled by 202 and 203 more economically.

FREIGHT CARS: The exact number of freight cars owned by AVI is a moot question in the absence of a company roster. We do know that AVI had the following as of 1921:

INTERURBANS

Here is the interior of AVI's finest car, No. 12. Its comfortable seats, big windows and solidity afforded the best in public transportation.

1	Flat car, 36'0" long	(251)
2	Freight & express trailers	(252-253) (1)
2	" " " "	(254-255) (2)
2	" " " "	(256-257) (3)
1	" " " "	(258) (4)
2	" " " "	(259-260) (5)
6	Rogers center dump cars	(401-406)
4	Side dump cars	(402, 406, 412, 420)
2	Refrigerator cars	(3000-3001) (6)

(1) Bought new 1912 from St. Louis Car Co.
(2) Bought from Wash. Water Power, Spokane
(3) Bought from Joliet & Eastern Railway
(4) Rebuilt by AVI from its original car 1
(5) Bought from Springfield, Mass.
(6) Bought from the Santa Fe, 1930

The above information has been furnished by Mr. Elmer Vallance and represents AVI's freight rolling stock to the best of his recollection. Discrepancies between his recollections and the Electric Railway Journal listings in the next column are indicated by a question mark.

CARS ORDERED: According to the annual lists of electric railway rolling stock orders as printed in Electric Railway Journal, AVI ordered cars as follows:

Year	Qty	Type		Length	Builder	No.
1910:	1	Int.	Closed	52'0"	Jewett	(1)
1911:	5	"	"	46'0"	St. Louis	(3-7)
	1	"	Freight	40'0"	"	(201)
1912:	3	"	Closed	46'0"	"	(8-10)
	2	"	Trail	40'0"	"	(252-3)
	1	"	Work	40'0"	"	(301)
	1	"	Flat	36'0"	"	(251)
1914:	1	City	Closed	30'0"	---	(51)
1915:	1	Int.	"	---		?
	1	"	Express	48'0"	St. Louis	(202)
	2	"	Exp. T.	42'0"		?
1916:	1	Int.	Closed	56'0"	Amer.	(12)
	1	"	Express	50'0"	"	(203)
1921:	1	City	Safety	22'4"	---	(100)

Omissions above are omissions by ERJ; in 1914 ERJ ceased listing builders. Numbers in parentheses refer to AVI's number on car.

Above: Car 3 has just crossed the Santa Fe near Newton and is heading for Van Arsdale in this 1937 photo taken from a Santa Fe diesel by Electromotive demonstrator Bill Johns.

Inset: Car 51 served the Bethel College line for many years and posed for many photos like this one. (MDI)

Below: Express motor 203 with three cars in tow has crossed the Seneca St. bridge in Wichita and is heading for Valley Center and Hutchinson.   (MDI)

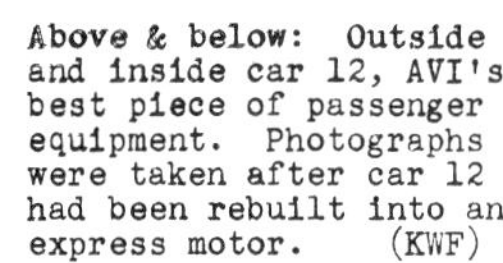

Above & below: Outside and inside car 12, AVI's best piece of passenger equipment. Photographs were taken after car 12 had been rebuilt into an express motor.   (KWF)

Here is car 5, at home alongside the Newton Station. Car 5 was made double-end for the Newton-Van Arsdale run to permit fast turn-arounds and to avoid tieing up the main line in wyeing operations.   (ES)

Entirely separate from AVI was the electric railway which still operates at KG&E's big power plant in Wichita. Above is shown the KG&E's electric locomotive as it looked in 1947. Purchased 1913, 48'11" long, four GE 50 motors, two K-14 controllers, 33" wheels and McGuire trucks; cost, $2100.   (KWF)

1

AVI's car number 1 was purchased new in 1910 from Jewett. This car was a very trim, attractive interurban combo mounted on big Baldwin trucks and was 52'0" in length.

Car 1 opened the line. While it was destined to play a minor role after newer and larger cars were received, none of them could claim similar distinction. As AVI's first car and as the first large electric car in Wichita, the 1-spot blazed a trail for all others to follow.

Unfortunately, not much can be learned of car 1 other than that data given above, plus the fact that it reportedly had Allis-Chalmers electrical equipment. It would be interesting to know why no similar cars were ordered---and how Jewett just happened to have this car available when AVI found itself faced with the dilemma of having the St. Louis Car Company's factory closed down at the very time it was needing cars 3-7 to open its line. Had St. Louis been able to deliver cars 3-7 on schedule, probably AVI would never have bought either car 1 or car First 2.

This car was rebuilt into freight trail car 263 and was scrapped in 1938; its siding was used as lining for car 12 when it was rebuilt into an express motor that year.

AVI's car 1 was this photogenic interurban car which combined a Jewett single-end composite body with Baldwin MCB trucks. Compare this attractive car with what it later became: freight trailer 258, shown below, left.

2

AVI had two cars numbered 2. First 2 was purchased from Cincinnati Car Company in 1910 and was a wooden passenger motor with Lorain electrical equipment.

First 2 was renumbered 11, probably about 1918; it later became line car 01 and was retired after a head on meet with car 4.

Above and below are photos of Second 2. In the photo above, the car is shown after removal from service; below, it wears AVI's red & cream paint and is in local service.

Above right: Line car 01, ex-11, ex-I 2; see also photo of car 11 on page 53.

2

Second 2 was purchased second hand from Michigan United Traction where it was the only car of its particular type, numbered MUT 68. It entered service in 1918.

This car was quite large and saw heavy use on AVI. Its distinguished career came to an end in 1936 when it jumped the track near 17th St. in Wichita and struck a pole, suffering considerable damage; it was never rebuilt. Its body today is at Bethel College in Newton.

GENERAL SPECIFICATIONS:

Builder: McGuire-Cummings, 1915
Type: Composite passenger-baggage combo
Length: 58'6" over buffers
Width: 8'8" over posts
Height: 13'0" over trolley board
Truck Centers: 33'10"
Trucks: McGuire-Cummings 70-A MCB
Truck Wheelbase: 6'6"
Motors: Four GE 205-E (80 hp each)
Gear Ratio: 21:53
Seats: 70 total, divided as follows:
       38 in main compartment
       16 in smoking section
       10 in baggage section
        6 collapsible chairs
Interior trim: Golden oak
Couplers: MCB radial

On Michigan United, this car was a double-ender; in photo at right (BN), it is easy to see how AVI closed up the old front door, making a motorman's cab out of the old exit.

3-10

Cars 3-10 were AVI's "Standard" type of interurban car. Cars 3-7 were built in 1911 by St. Louis Car Company, and the others followed a year later, also by St. Louis.

An excellent account of these cars was published in the "Electric Railway Journal" in its August 5, 1911, issue---from which we quote:

"The St. Louis Car Company has just completed five 46-ft. combination passenger, smoking & baggage cars for this railway company. These cars include some novel features of underframe design and interior arrangement. The general dimensions of the car are: Length over bumpers, 46'0"; length over vestibules, 45'2"; length inside main passenger compartment, 23'7½"; length inside rear vestibule, 4'0"; width inside between the wainscoting, 8'1¼"; width outside over the sheathing, 9'0"; extreme width, 9'2"; height from rail to sills, 3'5"; height from sill to trolley board, 10'0"; extreme height from rail to trolley board, 13'7"; minimum curve radius, 35'0".

"The new cars are divided into a baggage and smoking compartment seating 17 passengers, a main compartment seating 36 passengers, and a rear vestibule. Single end operation only has been provided for, and a motorman's cab has been set off from the forward left hand corner. Just behind this cab is a protected space for a Cooper hot water heater. The toilet room with its dry hopper is located on the rear platform. The cars have but one passenger entrance and it is at the right hand side of the rear vestibule. The bodies are mounted on St. Louis 23-B trucks with rolled steel wheels. The dimensions relating to the wheels and trucks are as follows: Diameter of wheels, 34"; tread, 3"; flange, 1"; wheelbase, 6'6"; and diameter of axles, 5½".

"The underframing is of novel construction. The side sills consist of two 9" 13¼ lb. channels laid back to back and spaced with wrought iron bars riveted between them. The channels have extensions over the upper flanges into which the side posts are bolted. The outside channel on the left side of the car extends in one piece from the center of the front bumper along the side, and around the rear bumper to the steps on the right hand side of the car. The outer channel on the right hand side of the car begins at the right hand end of the rear bumper, extends inwardly around the outline of the step opening and thence along the side of the car and around the front to join the other outer channel at the center of the front bumper, where they are spliced. These two channels completely encircle the outline of the car and are reinforced with gusset plates. The inside channels are bent around the end sills and carried toward the center of the car at each end to a point in line with the center sills, and thence extend forward and are connected with the buffer beams by gusset plates. The special forming of these inside channels, which are continuous from end to end of the car, affords substantial draft sills and center support for the buffer. The double channel iron side sills are covered on the bottom by 6" x 3/8" plates riveted to the lower flanges. The cross and end sills are of white oak trussed and tied to the inside channels. The truss plank is yellow pine, 1¼" x 10" in section, screwed and bolted to the posts and side channels.

"The body framing, which is of white ash ribbed and plated with long leaf yellow pine is sheathed on the outside with No. 16 sheet steel. The roof, which is of the steam coach type, is supported by continuous steel carlines anchored to post rods. The intervening roof framing is made of ash.

"There are 13 windows on each side of the body and one in the toilet room, located on the rear platform. The sashes are in two parts, the upper extending over two or three lower sashes to form a gothic window glazed with cathedral glass. The sashes are made

Here we see car 8 entering the Wichita Station in 1938. Note angularity of front end, a rare and distinguishing feature. In spite of their somewhat massive look, cars 3-10 were known to AVI men as the "little" cars.   (EV)

Car 4 at speed somewhere on AVI. When passenger business dwindled, AVI cars turned in respectable speed performances on their almost flat right of way. Cars 3-10 were reputedly good for 45 mph. (ES)

of mahogany designed to rise not less than 22". They are fitted with Edwards O-D 13 fixtures. The interior finish is mahogany in the passenger compartment and oak in the baggage and smoking compartment. All doors are made of solid mahogany, the rear end of the car having a sliding door in the center and the bulkhead between the interior compartments having a swinging door. The baggage compartment has a 36" sliding side door also equipped with a screen. The motorman's cab has a swinging outside door and a creep door leading to the baggage compartment. The interior of the rear vestibule is finished in mahogany and the outside of both vestibules is plated with No. 14 sheet steel.

"The single set of passenger steps at the right hand side of the rear vestibule has three oak treads covered with Empire safety treads. The steps are supported by steel hangers and risers. The step opening is covered with a trapdoor so arranged that it can not be lowered when the doors are open. Each car contains 18 St. Louis Car Company stationary seats in the passenger compartment, one of which is longitudinal. The seats have 36" cushions and 25" backs and are covered with plush. The six seats in the smoking compartment are also stationary and upholstered in rattan. This compartment has two wood drop seats in the baggage end. All the cross seats in the car have arm rests and are provided with corner grab handles, head rolls and adjustable foot rails.

"Some of the specialties included in the cars are as follows: Peacock handbrake with vertical wheels, Globe ventilator over saloon, MCB type couplers for radial operation,

Here is the 4-spot at Wichita Station about 1932, resplendent in its red and cream paint. This photograph, from the collection of Eugene Sabin, gives excellent detail of trucks, underframe and windows. Note blind spot at left front corner where motorman's cab was formerly located. (ES)

St. Louis continuous parcel racks and interior trimmings of bronze, Stempel fire extinguisher mounted on brackets, perforated rubber aisle matting, Westinghouse SME straight air brake equipment with No. 2 compressor and form J governor and 10" brake cylinder with alarm whistle, St. Louis trolley catcher and retriever. The front end of the car is fitted with an angle iron pilot so arranged that the front coupler will intercouple with another on a car of the same length and truck centers, and will be able to operate satisfactorily around curves of 40-foot radius."

GENERAL SPECIFICATIONS:

Builder: St. Louis Car Company, 1911-1912
Type: Composite passenger-baggage combo
Weight: 65,000 lbs.
Length: 46'0"
Width: 9'2"
Height: 13'7"
Trucks: St. Louis 23-B, 6'6", 34" wheels
Motors: Allis Chalmers; car 9 later got GE, and car 10 later demotorized.
Control: Westinghouse K-35 (not MU)
Seats: 52 (36 in main compartment)
Couplers: MCB radial
Brakes: Westinghouse SME
Compressor: Westinghouse No. 2

INDIVIDUAL HISTORIES:

3: Ran until 1938; body at 53rd & Broadway, Wichita.

4: Rebuilt after head-on accident with 01 in 1921. Headed last official passenger train, 1938. Body at 53rd & Broadway.

5: Made double end to serve Newton branch, 1922 (back up controller on rear platform, two trolleys, doors unchanged); ran backwards into Newton. Trailed No. 4 on final run, 1938. Body at 53rd & Broadway.

6: Wrecked and burned in head-on collision with freight train at 45 mph in 1928.

7: Ran until abandonment; body on U.S. 50S near Halstead.

8: Ran until abandonment; body at Bethel College, Newton, as dormitory.

9: Same as 8.

10: Rebuilt into a freight trailer; today body used as lunch car at Peabody, Kan.

NOTES: Although equipped with MCB couplers, these cars were incapable of working in multiple unit; couplers served to permit freight trailers to be hauled.
In 1917 all these cars were rebuilt; the motorman's door at left of front vestibule was closed, a single window put in in its rear, and cab was moved to the right hand side of the vestibule.

Car 7, as it looked about 1916. Here is shown the motorman's cab as it originally appeared. The awkward position of the motorman necessitated the use of mirrors to keep him informed of passengers' movements at the rear entrance and exit, located at the diametrically opposite corner of the car. Small wonder the cab was relocated! (BN)

11

Car 11 was a renumbering of car First 2. It was about 42'0" long, was entirely closed and did not have a baggage compartment. It was a true double-end car and may have been the Newton-Van Arsdale car before car 5.

12

From the Brill Magazine, June, 1917:

"An interurban car which embodies the latest developments in steel construction was delivered a few weeks ago to the AVI by the American Car Company. The car was designed by the builders to operate singly or with a trailer. In general the car is of steel construction with main, smoking and baggage compartments and equipped for single end operation. The design of the body, trucks and equipment conforms to MCB standards and implies a substantial track and roadbed with stations far enough apart to permit of high rates of speed. As a whole, the car forms a very complete interpretation of western ideas of interurban equipment and service. It is big, handsome, thoroughly modern and the roomy, bright and attractive interior with its well-planned compartments and comfortable seats will doubtless win additional traffic to this splendidly equipped and successful railway system.

"Steel beams, channels and angles connected at all joints with angle gussets constitute the underframe; the side and upper structure are also of steel with side posts of 2½ by ¼ in. tees. The corner posts and each alternate side post are double and all posts are riveted to the side sill, belt rail, side plate, letter panel and outside sheathing. Letter panels of No. 12 gauge steel are continuous around the sides and ends and are riveted to all posts; this steel is also employed for the sides below the windows and for the compartment partitions. Additional resistance against vertical strains is provided by inside and under trusses. The side walls below the windows are double with 2-3/4 in. air space between the outside steel sheathing and the inside lining which is of ¼" agasote.

"The floor is double and consists of 13/16 by 3¼ in. yellow pine with two thicknesses of water-proof building felt between. The lower floor is laid diagonally and secured to nailing sills bolted to the underframe; the top floor is laid lengthwise.

"Steel carlines support the plain arch roof, and wooden carlines, spaced at 10-in. centers, serve for the attachment of the roof sheathing and the ceiling. Trolley platforms are full length of the body and mats are provided to protect the roof ends from the trolleys.

"Each side of the car has 14 windows of twin type. The upper sashes are stationary and each extends across two lower sashes concealing with pressed prism plate glass the single side posts; the inside upper sashes are fitted with leaded cathedral glass. The lower sashes are arranged to raise between the double upper sashes.

"A swing door is provided in the center of the rear vestibule for train passage. Each side of the vestibule has a swing door and triple steps with trap door equipped underneath with a diagonally attached grab handle. The doors at the sides of the baggage compartment are of the sliding type with sliding screens to take their place in summer. The vestibule steps have ¼-in. steel plate hangers with tube binding; the treads are of oak with enameled nosings and covered with safety treads.

"All doors, sashes, moldings and small panels are made of cherry stained mahogany and the varnish rubbed to a dull finish. The ceiling is of cream color to increase the light by reflection. The main and the smoking compartments are finished in the same style and are separated by a glazed partition. Ash is used for the lining and stanchions of the baggage compartment and for the bars that form the side door pockets. The windows of this compartment are protected by iron rods spaced 3-in. apart.

"The motorman's cab in the right forward corner of the baggage compartment has a hinged entrance door and a drop window at the side. The toilet room at the rear of

Here is AVI's finest passenger interurban car, No. 12, as it appeared about 1934. It bears the red & cream paint, and is shown at Wichita Station. (ES)

After AVI abandoned passenger service in 1938, Car 12's windows were boarded up, its seats removed, and it ran thereafter as an express car.   (KWF)

the main compartment has a sidewall type of flush closet with overhead tank. A removable metal water cooler is placed in an alcove in the toilet room partition and arranged to keep the ice from coming in contact with the water in accordance with the laws of Kansas.

"In the main compartment the seats are of the Brill stationary-back type with head roll, bronze grab-handle, arm rest, foot rail and spring edge cushions; they are upholstered in dark green plush.

"Those in the smoking compartment are the same except they are upholstered in leather and four have reversible backs. Ash slat seats hinged to the side walls are provided in the baggage compartment.

"Included in the equipment of the car are a hot air heater located in the baggage compartment, eight ventilators in the roof, parcel racks, air whistle and gong, track sanders and MCB radial couplers.

"Brill trucks of the 27-MCB-2 type carry the car and are equipped with 34-in. rolled steel wheels."

This car closely resembles the Utah Idaho Central's 500-517 Class, although smaller.

<u>GENERAL SPECIFICATIONS:</u>

Builder: American Car Company, 1917
Type: Steel combination baggage-passenger
Weight: 79,000 lbs.
   Weight of Body: 34,000 lbs.
Length: 56'0"
Height: 13'4"
Width: 9'2"
Length Main Compartment: 25'7½"
Length Smoking Section: 11'0"
Length Baggage Section: 12'4½"
Length Rear Vestibule: 5'2½"
Width of Train Door: 30"
Width of Seats: 36" & 39"
Width of Aisle: 23¼"
Seats, Main Compartment: 34
Seats, Smoking Section: 16
Seats, Baggage Section: 6
Trucks: Brill 27-MCB-2
Journals: 4¼ x 8
Motors: Four GE 205-E (80 hp)
Gear Ratio: 21:53

After abandonment, the body of this car was sold to a private individual; today the body is used for feed storage at Bentley, Kansas.

INTERURBANS

15

Car 15 was a combination passenger and baggage motor, 45'0" long, built mostly of steel and having an arch roof.

Old-timers recall that cars 14 (101) and 15 were bought second hand from "a road in the Bluegrass Country---seems like Tennessee."

This car was mounted on Brill 27-MCB trucks and was equipped with Allis-Chalmers motors. Its lines in general indicate an early steel type of construction, perhaps about 1913.

AVI sold this car to the Northeast Oklahoma Railway at an unknown date.

51

Car 51 was the little city car used on the line from Newton to Bethel College during the Teens. Electric Railway Journal lists it as having been bought new in 1914; however, retired AVI men recall that one of the Wichita single-truckers was purchased to serve the Bethel line.

At any rate, this little deck roof single trucker was replaced by a Birney in 1921. 51 then supposedly was sold to the Southwest Interurban.

100

Car 100 was a Birney Safety car bought new by AVI in 1921. It was hoped by the use of this one-man car to make the Bethel Line a paying proposition, but such failed to materialize. With the abandonment of the Bethel Line in 1925, car 100 was sold to the Union Electric Railway of Coffeyville, Kansas, where it ran for many years.

102

Passenger trailer 102 was acquired in 1921 from the Washington Water Power Co. of Spokane, which had operated it on lines to Medical Lake and Cheney. The car was built by Brill about 1906 and probably was WWP 19.

Car 102 was fitted up as a somewhat more luxurious car than the AVI standard. Its open observation platform added dignity and authority to two-and-three-car trains.

In the photograph at the right, 102 is posed on the loop at Wichita Station about 1922. Enjoying the observation platform are three AVI officials of that day: a Mr. Morrison of the Traffic Department, Gen. Mgr. R. B. Campbell in center, and Superintendent Ailee Martin at right. Coupled ahead of 102 is trailer 101; compare with the photo above of this type car in later years on the Northeast Oklahoma Railway. Probably this photo of 102 and 101 showed AVI's high in passenger rolling stock; headed by motor 12, such a three-car train would have provided the Wichita-Hutchinson main line with the best limited service of which AVI was ever capable.

Car 102 was about 45 feet in length, and was mounted on Brill 27-E trucks.

Note in photo that train is looping in the wrong direction in order to get the morning light behind camera.

● Car 102 of the Northeast Oklahoma Railway (above) was formerly either AVI 15 or 101. In the above photo by Ray Hilner at Miami, the 102 was in service as a line car but comparatively unchanged from its passenger days.

101

Car 101 was first numbered AVI 14, but it was demotorized and renumbered 101 at an unknown date. In the photo below, it is coupled ahead of trailer 102.

This car was mounted on Brill 27-MCB trucks but had 33" wheels instead of 36" as car 15 had.

When 101 was sold to the Northeast Oklahoma Railway (Miami, Oklahoma), it was again motorized by AVI, getting Allis-Chalmers equipment.

Note that AVI was superstitious: never a 13.

Here is a view of AVI's Wichita Station taken from across the Arkansas River after Ackerman's Island had been removed. Note Broadview Hotel building, built in 1921 by many of AVI's backers.   (RH)

201

201 was AVI's first express motor. It was built by St. Louis Car Company in 1911 and was forty feet long. This car arrived before the extension into Newton was opened and is reputed to have been the first AVI car into that city under its own power.

Car 201 was of composite construction; it had a steel underframe, but the rest of the car was wood. It was mounted on St. Louis 23-B trucks and was double end, as were all AVI express motors.

AVI had a hard time making up its mind as to the end door on its express motors; 201's doors were at the right side of each end; 202's doors were non-existent; and 203 had doors at the left side.

After 203 went into service, 201 became the standby car and when line car 301 was wrecked, it was decided to rebuild 201 into the AVI's line car. This took place about 1917, according to old-timers. This car was retired in 1938.

GENERAL SPECIFICATIONS:

Builder: St. Louis Car Company, 1911
Type: Composite express motor
Length: 40'0"
Weight: 55,000 lbs. (estimated)
Motors: Four GE 217
Gear Ratio: 22:65
Trucks: St. Louis 23-B, 36" wheels
Brakes: Westinghouse automatic
Couplers: Radial, MCB type

202

In January, 1916, AVI purchased this express motor new from the St. Louis Car Co. at a price of $14,098.26. 202 was AVI's first heavy duty freight motive power, and it enabled AVI to increase greatly its freight business.

Car 202 was 48'0" long, weighed 70,000 pounds and was powered with four GE 205-E motors of 80 horsepower each. Although the total horsepower thus was normally rated at 320 horsepower, it theoretically was capable of exerting as high as 600 horsepower for short periods due to the unlimited supply of current from the overhead trolley and fixed voltage. This was a big step forward for AVI and made possible freight trains up to twelve cars in length. In fact, 202 was so successful that a very similar car of the same horsepower was ordered late the same year (see 203).

Cars 202 and 203 were AVI's workhorses; not only did they pull trains, but at the same time they carried up to 40,000 tons of freight inside. They were used in regular service between Wichita, Hutchinson and Newton daily except Sundays and holidays. The weight of their trains averaged 235 tons--- with a maximum of 400 tons and a minimum of 70 tons. Each car made a round trip daily, thus running up a daily total of 115.2 miles. Their average speed was approximately 20 mph with a maximum speed of 35 mph; it took them about 3½ hours to make a one-way run. This called for frequent accelerations, there being an average of fifteen stops per run plus speed restrictions of from 5 to 15 mph at certain street crossings and bridges. In addition, these cars performed switching at four different stations en route.

GENERAL SPECIFICATIONS:

Builder: St. Louis Car Company, 1916
Type: Composite express motor
Length: 48'0"
Weight: 70,000 lbs.
Motors: Four GE 205-E, 80 hp. each
Gear Ratio: 16:58
Trucks: Baldwin, 34" wheels
Brakes: Westinghouse automatic
Couplers: Radial, MCB type
Journals: 5 x 9

Here is line car 201 at Sedgwick in November, 1937. For a photo of 201 when it was younger, see front cover. Note that in the above photo, 201 has Baldwin trucks. (RH)

201 at Wichita Shops, 1937. (ES)　　　　202 at Wichita Station, 1937. (ES)

In this 1937 photo by Ray Hilner, 202 stands in the Wichita Station yard. Note front door placed on side rather than in end, as was done with 201 and 203. (RH)

Tractive effort exerted by 202 and 203 was as follows:

TE	250	300	400	600	1000	1500	17,000
MPH	29.8	28	25.5	22.3	18.3	15.9	10*

* Last figure is for the short haul up the Santa Fe overpass between Van Arsdale and Newton; this works out to approximately 500 horsepower with a 400 ton train at a minimum speed of 10 mph. This both 202 and 203 were capable of exerting for short periods. This grade was but a half mile long.

In 1934 car 202 (and 203) was considered for conversion to a self-propelled unit but the cost was prohibitive. It and 203 were scrapped after dieselization.

INTERURBANS

203

From the Brill Magazine, April, 1917:

"For use as an electric locomotive, as well as for carrying package freight and express matter, the AVI recently purchased from the American Car Company a 50-ft. baggage and express car mounted on Brill 27 MCB trucks. Because of the nature of the service for which it will be used, the car is built exceptionally strong so as to stand up.

"The car is built with straight-grained ash corner, end and side posts, each reinforced with a 5/8 inch rod extending from the top plate to the side sills. Each side sill is trussed with 1½ inch round rods upset at the ends and fitted with twin buckles for adjustment. The underframe is of steel throughout. The roof is of the arch type, the carlines of ash, reinforced with forged steel carlines. The roof is of poplar boards covered with canvas duck in one piece.

"At each side of the car in the center there is located a sliding door opening seven feet. These doors have narrow upper openings which are glazed. The motorman stands in the right hand corner of the vestibule, and in the left hand corner of each vestibule there is a swinging door, hinged on the corner posts and turning in."

This car was numbered 203 and was AVI's best box motor.

GENERAL SPECIFICATIONS:

Builder: American, 1916-17
Type: Composite box motor
Weight: 70,000 lbs.
    Weight of Body: 25,000 lbs.
Length: 50'0"
Height: 13'0"
Truck Centers: 32'4"
Width: 9'0"
Trucks: Brill 27-MCB
Wheels: 34"
Motors: Four GE 205-E (80 hp)
Gear Ratio: 16:58
Journals: 5 x 9
Cost: $14,983.04

In addition to performing the duties of a locomotive, AVI's express cars carried up to 40,000 lbs. of freight themselves.

In 1934, serious consideration was given to converting 203 into a self-propelled car but estimates received from car builders ran too high for AVI's pocketbook.

251

Car 251 was probably AVI's first freight car of any type. It was purchased in 1912 from the St. Louis Car Company along with six other cars (3 passenger motors, 2 passenger trailers and 1 work car).

251 was listed as being 36'0" long, and was mounted on St. Louis trucks. There is little reason to doubt that 251 was built at the same time as work car 301 for there was a marked similarity in these two pieces of equipment. Even after 301 was rebuilt and became 601, its underframe was almost identical with that of 251, as the photo at the right testifies.

251 served as AVI's snowplow in winter time. With a flange plow mounted at one end, its bed weighed down with rocks, and a stout locomotive pushing, 251 kept the line open and patrons happy.

Seldom was AVI tied up by snow. The level prairies made it much easier to control snowfall than in more mountainous areas.

Here is car 203, AVI's newest and best express motor. This car hauled the bulk of AVI freight, handling 350 tons trailing at speeds up to 25 mph. It was capable of making one round trip (115.2 miles) per eight hours with a train up to twelve cars in length. Note steel sides.

Here's proof that the flat plains of Kansas can get mighty cold in winter. Locomotive 601 (ex-301) pushes flat car 251 down the main line, removing any snow which the wind might have caused to drift onto the interurban's high iron. Note similarity of underframes of these two cars. (ES)

Another wintry scene is reproduced at the left: cars 12 and 203 in Wichita Station yard in the depth of winter. This was after 12 had been rebuilt into an express car. AVI's freight house appears in right background. Above it were located the trainmen's rooms, also used by the AVI Ladies' Auxiliary for their meetings. Waco Ave. is to rear of 203, as is also a portion of the large Broadview Hotel.

301

Car 301 was a combination work car and line car, as photo at right shows. It was purchased new from St. Louis Car Company in 1912 and was usually teamed with flat car 251 in construction days. Probably 301 was the first car into both Newton and Hutchinson.

301 had a steel underframe and wooden cab and bed. It was mounted on St. Louis trucks of a strengthened 23 design. It was equipped with a radial MCB coupler slotted to take a link.

This car was seriously damaged by fire in 1921 and was completely rebuilt, becoming electric locomotive 601.

601

In 1922, in the then-new Ackerman's Island Shops, AVI spent $15,638.37 under the supervision of Master Mechanic Vallance and got the formidable steel locomotive shown at right, below. Photos indicate that the main part of old 301 retained in the 601 was the heavy steel underframe. Trucks, body and electrical equipment were all new.

GENERAL SPECIFICATIONS:

```
Builder:    AVI, Ackerman's Island, 1922
Length:     40'0"
Weight:     100,000 lbs.
Motors:     Four GE 222C (110 hp. each)
Gear Ratio: 16:58
Wheels:     34"
Control:    K-34
Trucks:     Baldwin
```

601 was geared for speed rather than for high tractive effort. It was capable of hauling twelve freight cars at speeds up to 30 mph. According to Master Mechanic Vallance, 601 could haul an 800 ton train at 13½ mph. The bed of this locomotive was weighted with concrete.

At the time the 601 was constructed, AVI was hoping to get into the freight business in a big way. As things worked out, most of the company's freight was hauled by box motors 202 and 203, with 601 being used for heavy freight drags which moved perhaps once a week. After 1929, when 602 was bought, 601 saw even less service. It was not considered for conversion to diesel and it was scrapped in 1941.

602

Locomotive 602 was purchased new in April, 1929, from General Electric. It was a steel steeple cab freight motor of traditional GE design. It cost $25,896.57.

GENERAL SPECIFICATIONS:

```
Builder:  General Electric, Erie, Pa., 1929
Weight:   100,000 lbs.
Length:   35'9" (37'9" over couplers)
Width:    9'6"
Height:   13'0"
Motors:   Four GE 257 (135 hp. each)
Ratio:    16:65
Wheels:   36"
```

602 had a free running speed with a load of 350 tons of approximately 13.7 mph. Its motors had an hourly rating of 308 HP and a total horsepower in parallel of 640. Thus its forte was drag operation. It was considered for conversion to diesel in 1934.

The Valley Center oil field made 602 necessary to move bulk crude and supplies. AVI moved the first train of oil from Wright #1 in late 1928.

● Here we see work motor-line car 301 as it looked about 1916. This car was forty feet long and could carry long objects such as poles alongside its island cab. No information available as to electrical equipment.

At the left is a photo of 601 taken in 1939, showing the locomotive toward the end of its life. Below is AVI's builder's photo, taken in 1923. Compare this photo with that of 301 above and note that only the underframe is recognizable. Notable characteristics of this freight motor were its square, angular lines and its multiplicity of windows in the cab. Its motors drew 159 amperes when turning over at 625 rpm @ 600 volts. (ES)

Steel steeple cab locomotive 602 was AVI's finest piece of rolling stock. Purchased new in April, 1929, from General Electric, it weighed 100,000 lbs. and could haul trains of twenty cars, although not at high speed. After dieselization this motor was sold to the Chicago, North Shore & Milwaukee Railroad which renumbered it 457. It is still in service on the North Shore as of 1956. (EV)

At right we see the two refrigerator cars, 3000 and 3001, at the Wichita freight house. Bought used in 1930, the reefers were more or less standard with the exception of their draft gear which was too light to permit their use in interchange service. (RH)

Below is a view of the Wichita Station in the fall of 1938, with the Broadview Hotel in the background (built over the freight house). At the right is car 12 after having been rebuilt into an express motor; passenger service was abandoned on August 1, 1938, and the rebuilding of this car took about six weeks. At left are 3001 & 203. (MDI)

Above is interurban freight trailer 252; it was a light car, not suitable for interchange.

At the left is interurban freight trailer 257, a semi-steel car capable of high speed service. Note its trucks---St. Louis 23-Bs---and 36" wheels.

NEWTON DIVISION

South Bound---Read Down   North Bound---Read Up

N-6	N-6	N-6	N-5	N-5	N-5	Miles from Newton	STATIONS AND SIDINGS	Miles from Van Arsdale	N-5	N-5	N-5	N-6	N-6	N-6
132	130	128	126	124	122		TRAIN NUMBERS		123	125	127	129	131	133
Daily Leave	Daily Leave	Daily Leave	Daily Leave	Daily Leave	Daily Leave		STATIONS AND SIDINGS		Daily Arrive	Daily Arrive	Daily Arrive	Daily Arrive	Daily Arrive	Daily Arrive
P. M.	P. M.	P. M.	P. M.	A. M.	A. M.				A. M.	A. M.	P. M.	P. M.	P. M.	P. M.
8:30	6:10	4:00	1:30	11:00	8:30	.0	NEWTON 2.8	6.0	9:05	11:35	2:05	4:35	6:45	9:05
8:37	6:17	4:07	1:37	11:07	8:37	2.8	THEIS 211 Ft. 3.2	3.2	8:58	11:28	1:58	4:28	6:38	8:58
8:45	6:25	4:15	1:45	11:15	8:45	6.0	VAN ARSDALE	.0	8:50	11:20	1:50	4:20	6:30	8:50
P. M.	P. M.	P. M.	P. M.	A. M.	A. M.				A. M.	A. M.	P. M.	P. M.	P. M.	P. M.
Arrive	Arrive	Arrive	Arrive	Arrive	Arrive				Leave	Leave	Leave	Leave	Leave	Leave
132	130	128	126	124	122		TRAIN NUMBERS		123	125	127	129	131	133
N-6	N-6	N-6	N-5	N-5	N-5		RUN NUMBERS		N-5	N-5	N-5	N-6	N-6	N-6

WICHITA—HUTCHINSON
MAIN LINE

East and South Bound---Read Down   North and West Bound---Read Up

H-4	W-3	H-4	H-2	W-1	H-2	W-1	Miles from Hutchinson	STATIONS AND SIDINGS	Miles from Wichita	W-1	W-1	H-2	H-2	W-3	H-4	H-4
32	30	28	26	24	22	20		TRAIN NUMBERS		21	23	25	27	29	31	33
Daily Leave	Daily Leave	Daily Leave	Daily Leave	Daily Leave	Daily Leave	Daily Ex. Sun. Lv.		STATIONS AND SIDINGS		Daily Ex. Sun. Ar.	Daily Arrive	Daily Arrive	Daily Arrive	Daily Arrive	Daily Arrive	Daily Arrive
P. M.	P. M.	P. M.	P. M.	A. M.	A. M.	A. M.				A. M.	A. M.	A. M.	P. M.	P. M.	P. M.	P. M.
7:55	5:35	3:25	12:55	10:25	7:55		.0	HUTCHINSON (C.R.I.&P.RY. CROSSING) 1.4	51.6		9:45	12:15	2:45	5:15	7:25	9:45
7:59	5:39	3:29	12:59	10:29	7:59		1.4	LORAINE AVE. .5	50.2		9:40	12:10	2:40	5:10	7:20	9:40
8:01	5:41	3:31	1:01	10:31	8:01		1.9	CAREY LAKE H. & N. Conn. .4	49.7		9:38	12:08	2:38	5:08	7:18	9:38
8:02	5:42	3:32	1:02	10:32	8:02		2.3	STRAWBOARD 291 Ft. .5	49.3		9:37	12:07	2:37	5:07	7:17	9:37
8:03	5:43	3:33	1:03	10:33	8:03		2.8	SALT MINE A. V. I. Track 68 Ft. / Salt Mine Track 2.6	48.8		9:36	12:06	2:36	5:06	7:16	9:36
8:08	5:48	3:38	1:08	10:38	8:08		5.4	STRANDBERG 205 Ft. 1.6	46.2		9:31	12:01	2:31	5:01	7:11	9:31
8:11	5:51	3:41	1:11	10:41	8:11		7.0	COOPER 306 Ft. 2.3	44.6		9:28	11:58	2:28	4:58	7:08	9:28
8:14	5:54	3:44	1:14	10:44	8:14		9.3	SMYTH 235 Ft. 2.2	42.3		9:25	11:55	2:25	4:55	7:05	9:25
8:17	5:57	3:47	1:17	10:47	8:17		11.5	MORRISON 325 Ft. 2.1	40.1		9:22	11:52	2:22	4:52	7:02	9:22
8:21	6:01	3:51	1:21	10:51	8:21		13.6	BURRTON SIDING A. V. I. Track 55 Ft. / Frisco Conn. .1	38.0		9:18	11:48	2:18	4:48	6:58	9:18
8:22	6:02	3:52	1:22	10:52	8:22		13.7	BURRTON 2.6	37.9		9:17	11:47	2:17	4:47	6:57	9:17
8:26	6:06	3:56	1:26	10:56	8:26		16.3	BELL Double End Sdg. 801 Ft. 1.6	35.3		9:13	11:43	2:13	4:43	6:53	9:13
8:29	6:09	3:59	1:29	10:59	8:29		17.9	ARMSTRONG Double End Sdg. 1460 Ft. 2.5	33.7		9:10	11:40	2:10	4:40	6:50	9:10
8:34	6:14	4:04	1:34	11:04	8:34		20.4	WHITE 300 Ft. 2.7	31.2		9:05	11:35	2:05	4:35	6:45	9:05
8:40	6:20	4:10	1:40	11:10	8:40		23.1	HALSTEAD Double End. Sdg. 762 Ft. / House Track 247 Ft. 2.5	28.5		9:00	11:30	2:00	4:30	6:40	9:00
8:45	6:25	4:15	1:45	11:15	8:45		25.6	MISSION Double End. Sdg. 750 Ft. 2.5	26.0		8:55	11:25	1:55	4:25	6:35	8:55
8:50	6:30	4:20	1:50	11:20	8:50		28.1	VAN ARSDALE Double End. Sdg. 572 Ft. 1.0	23.5		8:50	11:20	1:50	4:20	6:30	8:50
8:52	6:32	4:22	1:52	11:22	8:52		29.1	BRIGGS 319 Ft. 2.0	22.5		8:47	11:17	1:47	4:17	6:27	8:47
8:55	6:35	4:25	1:55	11:25	8:55		31.1	HALL 397 Ft. 2.7	20.5		8:44	11:14	1:44	4:14	6:24	8:44
9:01	6:41	4:31	2:01	11:31	9:01		33.8	SEDGWICK Double End. Sdg. 920 Ft. / Spur Track 256 Ft. 2.6	17.8		8:39	11:09	1:39	4:09	6:19	8:39
9:06	6:46	4:36	2:06	11:36	9:06		36.4	CONGDON 373 Ft. 2.2	15.2		8:33	11:03	1:33	4:03	6:13	8:33
9:09	6:49	4:39	2:09	11:39	9:09		38.6	FERGUSON 350 Ft. 1.7	13.0		8:30	11:00	1:30	4:00	6:10	8:30
9:13	6:53	4:43	2:13	11:43	9:13	7:13	40.3	VALLEY CENTER Wye 176 Ft. .1	11.3	7:10	8:27	10:57	1:27	3:57	6:07	8:27
9:14	6:54	4:44	2:14	11:44	9:14	7:14	40.4	ST. L. & S. F. RY. CROSSING Double End. Sdg. 896 Ft. 1.5	11.2	7:09	8:26	10:56	1:26	3:56	6:06	8:26
9:17	6:57	4:47	2:17	11:47	9:17	7:17	41.9	GOODRICH 860 Ft. 1.9	9.7	7:07	8:23	10:53	1:23	3:53	6:03	8:23
9:21	7:01	4:51	2:21	11:51	9:21	7:21	43.8	INTERURBAN PLACE Double End. Sdg. 628 Ft. 1.2	7.8	7:03	8:19	10:49	1:19	3:49	5:59	8:19
9:23	7:03	4:53	2:23	11:53	9:23	7:23	45.0	FOREST PARK Sand Boat Track D'ble End. Sdg. 1.3	6.6	7:02	8:17	10:47	1:17	3:47	5:57	8:17
9:26	7:06	4:56	2:26	11:56	9:26	7:26	46.3	WALNUT GROVE 190 Ft. 1.8	5.3	6:59	8:14	10:44	1:14	3:44	5:54	8:14
9:30	7:10	5:00	2:30	12:00	9:30	7:30	48.1	21st STREET 248 Ft. 2.6	3.5	6:55	8:10	10:40	1:10	3:40	5:50	8:10
9:36	7:16	5:06	2:36	12:06	9:36	7:36	50.7	WATER WORKS 380 Ft. .6	.9	6:49	8:04	10:34	1:04	3:34	5:44	8:04
9:38	7:18	5:08	2:38	12:08	9:38	7:38	51.3	MIDLAND VALLEY Double End. Sdg. 277 Ft. .3	.3	6:47	8:02	10:32	1:02	3:32	5:42	8:02
9:40	7:20	5:10	2:40	12:10	9:40	7:40	51.6	WICHITA (M.O.P.RY. CROSSING)	.0	6:45	8:00	10:30	1:00	3:30	5:40	8:00
P. M.	P. M.	P. M.	P. M.	P. M.	A. M.	A. M.				A. M.	A. M.	A. M.	P. M.	P. M.	P. M.	P. M.
Arrive	Arrive	Arrive	Arrive	Arrive	Arrive	Arrive				Leave	Leave	Leave	Leave	Leave	Leave	Leave
32	30	28	26	24	22	20		TRAIN NUMBERS		21	23	25	27	29	31	33
W-3	W-3	H-4	W-1	W-1	H-2	W-1		RUN NUMBERS		W-1	W-1	H-2	W-1	W-3	H-4	W-3

(At VAN ARSDALE the junction run and train numbers are repeated: south bound 33 31 29 27 25 23; north bound 22 24 26 28 30 32.)

Note 1:—When passing train at meeting point, conductor of the train taking siding will signal approaching train to proceed, provided track is clear and motorman on approaching train will not pass over switch at meeting point until signalled to approach by conductor of opposing train.

Note 2:—Telephones are stationed at all passing points except Burrton siding, Strawboard and double end siding, Sedgwick.

Note 3:—Local trains will stop at point designated by sign as point at which local trains will stop to receive and discharge passengers.

Note 4:—All passenger trains will stop at points at which ticket offices are maintained to receive and discharge passengers.

Note 5:—Time used—From 12:01 A. M. to 12 noon is A. M. time— From 12:01 P. M. to 12 midnight is P. M. time.

Note 6:—Distances shown at sidings are from clearance post to clearance post or from clearance post to end of track.

Note 7:—Crews on Run W-1, train 27, and Run H-2, train 26, will swing at Van Arsdale at 1:50 P. M.

Note 8:—Crews on Run W-3, train 33, and Run H-4, train 32, will swing at Van Arsdale at 8:50 P. M.

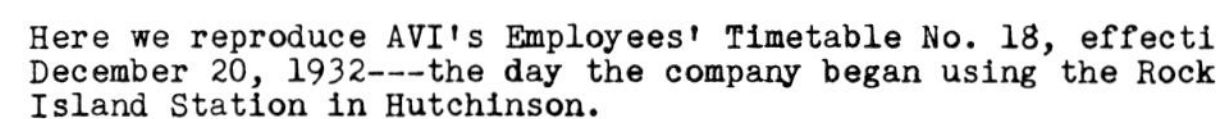
Here we reproduce AVI's Employees' Timetable No. 18, effective December 20, 1932---the day the company began using the Rock Island Station in Hutchinson.

RED-IVORY CARS FOR INTERURBAN PASSENGERS NOW

Select Loud Colors as Means to Reduce Accidents on Electric Line Here

REPORT BUSINESS GOOD

With a record breaking year for traffic movements just completed, the last two months of which showed twice the volume of the same months the year before, Robert B. Campbell, president of the Arkansas Valley Interurban company, issued yesterday a statement which expressed no fear of the coming year for the electric line.

"Passenger traffic still continues unsuccessfully to compete with automobiles. For the past four years this business has suffered considerably, but the drop in 1927 below 1926 was less than ever before. This, we believe, indicates that the passenger business is becoming stabilized," he said.

However, Mr. Campbell pointed out that this year is being started with the expenditure of $15,000 for the improvement of passenger service. Six rebuilt passenger cars will be in the service shortly. All the cars have been repainted.

"Our cars were formerly of the 'Pullman green' color," he said. "But if I wanted any car to be inconspicuous I'd paint it just that color to blend with the landscape. But that's not the intention. The A. V. I. cars should be evident a mile away to reduce accidents, and I'm proud to announce one of the loudest color schemes I could lay my hands on. In a short time the public will ride in an interurban car the lower portion of which is a flaming red and the upper an ivory color."

Freight traffic last year showed a nice increase, Mr. Campbell said. Oil movements were particularly good. Livestock reports showed the interurban handled 1,299 head of horses and mules during the year. There were 296 carloads of livestock shipped over the short electric line. Milk shipments, package freight and express movements for the year were about the same as usual, Mr. Campbell stated.

"Our line is in good condition. Over its mileage during the past year some 25,000 ties were placed and every inch of the roadbed is in good condition. We expected to have about the same tie renewal program this year," he said.

—Wichita "Eagle" Jan. 11, 1928

...BAN COMPANY ...REASES BUSINESS

...of interest to our readers that regardless of auto and other methods of transpassenger and freight the Arkansas Valley Interurban Railway Company has shown [an incre]ase for the month of October over the corresponding month of 1927.

During October of this year 873 passengers from this city rode on the Interurban as compared to 742 for October 1927. The total amount of freight handled in October was 2,-338,032 pounds and a year ago it totaled 730,566, or 20 carloads in October 1928 as against six carloads in October 1927, and the receipts for the same period showed a nice increase.

New improvements of the Company as well as others were responsible for the large increase in the volume of freight handled in October as five carloads of cement or 278,160 pounds were carried while 43,172 pounds of steel and 24,000 pounds of road machinery were hauled over the A. V. I. For the same month a year ago none of the last three items mentioned were transported here.

The increase in passengers may be due to the reduced fares the road has offered for various attractions in Hutchinson or Wichita which were of local interest and George M. Anderson, local agent, is making an effort to secure reduced rates to those cities each week-end and the company may decide to do so. Interurban officials are anxious to maintain good service and there is no doubt but what they will continue to give the best possible in the future as they have in the past.

—Halstead "Independent" November 22, 1928

Chapter 5

Passenger Operations

<u>LIMITED SERVICE:</u> AVI's passenger operations were distinguished by its high speed limiteds which ran from 1918 to 1925. These provided excellent service to business men and shoppers, but were not so good for the farmers. Here, digested from employees' timetables, is what AVI ran in the way of limited-stop service during its heyday:

The general picture was: April, 1918, two Limiteds each way daily, taking 110 minutes for the 52.3 miles between Wichita and Hutchinson. July, 1918, three each way, 110 min.; February, 1920, five each way, 110 minutes; January 1922, four each way, 102 minutes, the fastest time; March, 1924, had five each way, taking 105 minutes. Effective March 22, 1925, all Limiteds eliminated.

To break this down: effective April 14, 1918, a Limited left Wichita at 7:10 AM, arriving Hutchinson at 9:15; the car left Hutchinson at 9:30 AM, arriving Wichita at 11:20; it left Wichita at 3:00 PM, arriving at 4:50; and left Hutchinson at 5:15, arriving 7:05. This service was undoubtedly provided by car 12, which then was AVI's only car with big motors.

On July 28, 1918, Limited service was increased and a second high speed car entered service, undoubtedly car Second 2; this gives us our only clue as to date II 2 went into AVI service after having been purchased from Michigan United. **Limiteds left Wichita at 6:40 AM, 12:00 noon and 4:00 PM; they left Hutchinson at 6:30 AM, 11:50 AM and 3:50 PM.** Probably 12 was based at Wichita, II 2 at Hutchinson.

A new high in Limiteds was reached effective February 1, 1920. On that date, AVI began the following Limited schedule: Leave Wichita at 9:00 AM, 12:00 noon, 2:30 PM, 4:30 PM and 8:00 PM. Limiteds left Hutchinson at 8:50 AM, 11:50 AM, 2:20 PM, 4:20 PM and 7:50. This could still be provided by but two cars.

As of January 15, 1922, Limiteds were cut to four, leaving Wichita at 9:30 AM, 12:15 PM, 2:30 PM and 4:20 PM; they left Hutchinson at 9:15 AM, 12:00 noon, 2:15 PM and 4:15 PM.

This remained in force until March 15, 1924, when a late Limited was added at either terminal. Leave Wichita 9:30 AM, 12:00 noon, 2:30 PM, 4:30 PM and 8:00 PM. Leave Hutchinson at 9:20 AM, 11:45 AM, 2:20 PM, 4:20 PM, and 7:50 PM.

In 1925 all Limiteds were gone. Although AVI endeavored to give the best possible service by scheduling Limited trains, a certain amount of opposition developed. AVI served both the city dweller and the farmer. The business man and the shopper naturally liked fast, through service to the opposite city. The farmer and his wife wanted frequent cars

Passenger motor 4, resplendent in red and cream paint, is seen here crossing the Big Arkansas River from Ackerman's Island about 1933. This view looks west from the Wichita Station loop. (BN)

to their nearest crossroads stop. AVI could not please both. The only way it could have made both factions happy was by sending out a local ten minutes after each Limited; this was unfortunately economically impossible. AVI endeavored to strike a happy medium by alternating Limiteds with locals during the middle of the day, and concentrating on locals during morning and evening rush hours. This meant that more than one farmer missed a local by a few minutes and then was forced to sit for as much as two hours before a car would stop for him. Small wonder AVI lost out to the Model T!

AVI's timetables show a fascinating situation at Hutchinson in late afternoon. A Limited from Wichita was due in at 4:20 in 1920---and was due out also at 4:20. This

would have been a neat trick if the timetable was actually adhered to and if it was, AVI reached perfection in car utilization. In 1922 this was changed so that it arrived at 4:12 and left at 4:15---still a fine showing. In 1924, the car came in at 4:18 and left at 4:20. That particular car just didn't like Hutchinson!

Limiteds stopped at all timetable stations and in addition at 21st & Mascott St., Wichita, and at Ave. A & Main St., Hutchinson.

On the Main Line, all locals had to take the siding with Limiteds holding the high iron.

Limiteds did not consist of but the high speed motor car. Trailers 101 and 102 were added as the need arose. We have no proof of it---but in the event either 12 or II 2 were out of service temporarily, the only other cars equipped with big motors and able to meet the schedule were express motors 202 and 203. It may be possible that they were called upon to pinch hit occasionally.

LOCAL SERVICE: Local service on the Main Line was the backbone of AVI's passenger service. It started with 13 daily round trips between Wichita and Hutchinson. Running down the years, we find:

1918: 9 r-t, plus 1 r-t Wichita-Valley Cent.
1918: 11 r-t, 1 r-t Wichita-Valley Center.
1920: 9 r-t, plus 1 Valley Center to Wichita.
1922: 9 r-t, 1 r-t Wichita-Valley Center.
1923: 8 round trips.
1924: 9 round trips.
1925: 13 r-t, no Ltds., 1 r-t Wich-Val C.
1932: 6 round trips.
1937: 6 round trips.
1938, July 31st: Passenger service quit.

NEWTON DIVISION: The Newton Division consisted of a six-mile line extending from a junction with the Main Line at Van Arsdale to the city of Newton. For most of AVI's life, the Newton Division was served exclusively by a car which connected with Main Line trains, making a physical transfer necessary for patrons to and from Newton. Such patrons were sold a two-stub ticket for collection on the two passenger cars they would ride. A Newton business man who bought a round-trip ticket to Wichita or Hutchinson (saving 10% over the cost of two one-way fares) had to hand a four-stub ticket to the first AVI conductor.

A fairly comprehensive study of Newton service is possible for the years 1918-1924 from timetables loaned by Elmer Vallance, Ailee Martin and Kenneth W. Fry. The following digest of the Newton service is from these timetables, plus a 1932 and a 1936 timetable:

As of April 14, 1918 Newton was served by 13 locals from Van Arsdale, 12 locals to Van Arsdale, and two through trips to and from Wichita. The through cars left Newton at 6:10 AM and 1:35 PM, and left Wichita at 12:00 noon and 5:30 PM. These made the 29.3 miles in 75 minutes. Locals needed 15 minutes to and from Van Arsdale, 6 miles away.

On July 28, 1918, a new timetable went into effect, eliminating all through cars but giving Newton 14 locals to and from Van Arsdale.

The timetable dated January 15, 1922, has 13 locals to and from Van Arsdale. In addition, one through car left Wichita at 10:30 PM, arriving in Newton at 11:40; then it left Newton at 12:05 AM for Valley Center, arriving there at 12:50 AM and tieing up for the night, leaving there at 7:00 AM as the Wichita commuter car.

On June 25, 1922, Newton again lost its sole through car, being served by the usual 13 locals each way to Van Arsdale.

On March 4, 1923, Newton was given a thru car to Wichita, leaving at 6:30 AM and arriving Wichita at 7:35; returning, the car left Wichita at 5:30 PM and arrived in Newton at 6:40 PM. A dozen locals to and from Van Arsdale completed the picture.

On March 19, 1924, Newton had 14 trips each way to and from Van Arsdale.

On March 22, 1925, 17 trips, Van Ars.

On December 20, 1932, six trips to and from Van Arsdale.

This schedule remained in effect throughout the closing years of passenger operation. Finally, when riders dropped to almost zero, AVI asked and got permission to abandon passenger service---August 31, 1938.

Car 5 was made double end for use on the Newton Division and was that branch's usual car for many years. Car 5 was not given an altered body---it continued to have but one door---used alike for entrance and exit, no matter in which direction the car was headed.

● AVI's high speed interurban #12 is shown here as it passed through Sedgwick in 1937. It was November, and in this next-to-last year of AVI passenger service, #12 had a slim consist on board. The end was not far away. (RH)

The 5 also hauled freight cars, picking up a car at Van Arsdale left there by the mid-day local freight and returning the car the next day.

CREWS: From a study of employees' timetables, it appears as though AVI had a need of a maximum of six passenger crews at any one time. This was divided as follows:

Four crews worked the main line, putting in roughly an eight hour day. One crew put in eight hours on the Newton Division, and an extra crew handled the Valley Center commuter car. At about 4:00 PM these crews got relieved by others.

To understand the average days' work put in by a typical AVI crew, let us examine the crew assignments in effect in 1919. There are eight Run Numbers: D-1, D-2, D-3, D-4, L-6, L-7, L-8 and L-9 listed for through passenger service on the Main Line. There is one extra crew assignment, X-1 and X-2, taking care of the morning and evening car in the Valley Center commuter service. And there is a crew handling the Newton car with a D-5 Run Number and an L-10 Run Number.

Here is the assignment of crew D-3 for a typical day:

Lv Hutchinson 5:30 AM; arr. Wichita 7:42.
Lv. Wichita   8:00 ; arr. Hutch. 10:15.
Lv. Hutchinson 10:35 ; arr. Wichita 12:50.
Lv. Wichita   1:20 PM; arr. Hutch. 3:35.

On the Main Line, two crews worked out of Wichita and two out of Hutchinson. When the evening crews came on (L-6 to L-9) business did not require so many runs so they traded cars at Van Arsdale on their last runs, enabling Wichita men to sleep in Wichita and Hutchinson men to sleep at home also.

AVI continued the practise of Wichita RR. & Light Company in refering to day runs as "D" and late runs as "L".

Passenger crews and freight crews worked in a common pool.

FARES & TICKETS: AVI fares averaged about 2¢ per mile for a one-way ticket, 1.8¢ for a round trip. All passengers purchased tickets to ride; these were sold at the various stations on the line. Where a patron boarded at a shelter house

● Mixed trains were common on AVI in the Thirties. Here is car 4 hauling interurban freight trailer 257 at Hutchinson in 1937. (RH)

AVI used shelters like this to protect waiting passengers from the elements.

stop, he paid the conductor (who computed and collected the amount due) and received a cash fare receipt.

AVI patrons could purchase joint steam road tickets at AVI stations if they so desired. AVI agents had Western tariff books and were permitted to sell tickets originating on AVI and continuing on the steam lines to any destination in the United States.

Five types of tickets were sold: round trip (good for thirty days), Sunday, Special, Scrip, and Half Fare. Baggage was carried free on round trip tickets, but not on other types. Sunday and Special tickets were at the excursion rate; Scrip was for commuters and Half Fare was for children.

SPECIAL MOVEMENTS: AVI was quick to realize that special movements could mean the difference between profit and loss. It ran special trains as often as it could, and memories of such movements are green in the minds of old-timers today.

For instance, twice a year the State of Kansas held teachers' institutes; teachers traveled via AVI three-car specials if such an institute happened to be held on an on-line city. Every August, Halstead held an Old Settlers Picnic in a large shady park on the east bank of the Little Arkansas River just north of town; AVI handled large crowds to this event from 1914 on. In September, the Kansas State Fair was held in the large fairgrounds in the northern part of Hutchinson, complete with elaborate exhibits and a lively Midway; AVI brought thousands to the city where they transferred to the city cars. Wichita staged the Wheat Show every October in that city's huge Forum Building; the big stage shows were the outstanding live entertainment of the region and AVI patrons were deposited but a half mile from the Forum.

AVI did a good business in transporting high school and college rooters to and from athletic events. Wichita had the Friends University and Fairmont College. Newton had Bethel College and Hutchinson later established a large junior college. But as early as 1910, a tremendous rivalry was in full swing among high schools of the area. Among the sports which brought dollars to AVI were basketball, football, track and tennis. AVI special cars assisted in the triumphs and the despairs of the winning and losing team athletes and fans. The chartered cars were often decorated with the banners of the various schools and, of course, determined victory slogans.

Wichita's Riverside Park, Hutchinson's Carey Park and Newton's Athletic Park also proved good revenue sources for AVI. Each park was on a stream so fishing, swimming and boating were popular; Wichita's also had a sizeable zoo. Another popular attraction was Classen's Grove, a shaded spot between Newton and Van Arsdale; this was especially noted for its fine picnic grounds and was popular for club, company and family affairs. In the early days, AVI pushed a beautiful spot four miles above Wichita, Sullivan's Dam, as a fishing, boating and picnic spot.

ACCIDENTS: It was inevitable that AVI would have accidents, but fortunately none of them were of a major nature.

Perhaps the worst occurred on June 27, 1930, at Armstrong Siding east of Halstead, when passenger motor 6 ran through an open switch and hit the rear tank car of a freight which had taken the siding to let the passenger pass. The passenger car was badly telescoped and was never rebuilt.

Another time an early morning head-on collision occurred on the AVI when a motorman was blinded by the sun and ran into the line car; no passengers were injured and the passenger motor was later rebuilt.

A third incident which could have been a disaster took place when an axle broke under a speeding car; although the front truck turned crosswise beneath the car, Motorman Tom Newman was able to stop the car without injury to any of its fifty passengers.

Grade crossing accidents were much more macabre. As good roads gridironed Kansas, AVI found it had more grade crossings than miles of line. New drivers might stall on the track and panic at the sight of an approaching interurban car. At intervals papers of the area carried headline stories of another motorist killed or injured at an AVI grade crossing. One accident happened thusly: A Mrs. J. Murphy of Lawrence was coming to pay a visit to her sister who lived in Paxton. Upon leaving the Santa Fe at Halstead Mrs. Murphy phoned to ask her sister if she should take the AVI to Paxton; the husband, however, decided he would bring his sister-in-law home in style so left in his auto for Halstead. In the meantime, the wife began fixing a fine Harvey County dinner. Mr. Armstrong picked up his sister-in-law at Halstead and, returning, turned south at Paxton crossing. He crossed both tracks of the Santa Fe and was on the AVI track when his car was struck and demolished by an interurban he had failed to see. He and Mrs. Murphy were killed instantly. Paxton crossing saw frequent accidents. Another bad crossing was 29th St., north of Wichita. One accident there involved a transient laborer who, with his boss beside him, decided to race the boss' Model T against an AVI interurban. The Model T lost, crashing into the side of the car, breaking its air line which stopped it in about two hundred feet. Motorman Procious and Conductor Meek hastened back to render what aid they could to the man with the crushed head who liked to live dangerously.

RULES & REGULATIONS: The following rules and regulations have been selected from the AVI's official handbook distributed to all conductors & motormen. This pocket-sized paper-bound booklet contained 56 pages. Our copy was loaned by Mr. Ailee Martin, formerly General Superintendent of AVI:

16: The motorman is in charge of the car and is held responsible for the safe running of the car and for the proper operation of the car and its machinery and for running the car according to schedule. The conductor is in charge of the passengers and is held responsible for the safety and convenience of the passengers and for the collection and proper accounting of fares.

27: Cars must never be run ahead of schedule time, but must pass time-points and leave terminals promptly on time unless unavoidably delayed.

28: All relief changes will be made at such car barns and at such places as may be designated by bulletin from time to time. If one of the relief crew fails to report, the dispatcher or barn foreman must be notified and the run continued until a relief is provided. A car must never be run without its complete crew.

29: Cars must be brought to a full stop, at a safe distance (not less than 20 feet), approaching unprotected steam railroad crossings at grade. At sidings and spurs motormen will look both ways on steam railroad track and if safe to proceed will call for bell from conductor and after getting same will proceed over the crossing. At main line crossings conductor will go ahead over the crossing and if safe to proceed will give the "come ahead" signal which the motorman will acknowledge with the gong or the whistle before proceeding. At crossings protected by flagmen, accept signals from them instead of the conductor going over ahead of the car. At interlocking and derailing crossings motormen will be governed entirely by mechanical signals.

33: The motorman or conductor of any disabled car, withdrawn from the main track, must remain with the car until relieved by proper authority.

40: In the event of a blockade of cars by any cause, all cars in such blockade must not be started at one time, but only singly and at such intervals as will not burden the power house. Cars having even numbers will start as soon as power comes on; cars with odd numbers will start after one minute.

46: When taking cars out of the barn, conductors and motormen must thoroughly inspect cars for defects, test air and hand brakes, controllers, circuit breakers, heaters, registers, seats, doors, etc., to make sure all is in working order.

70: Conductor must be careful to see that register rings each fare and that the dial shows it.

74: When passing a church during the hours of service, and at all times when passing a hospital, do not use current and do not ring the gong unless necessary.

116: Single interurban cars or trains must always carry front and rear markers, target in front and flag on rear end by day, lamps by night, headlight in front by night, and proper destination signs at all times when in service. A regular car with car following will display "F" target by day, a red light by night; a regular car alone will display "R" target by day, a green light at night; the last following car of a regular train will display an "R" target by day, a green light by night; an extra car will display an "X" target by day, a white light by night; an extra car with a car following will display an "F" target by day, a red light by night; the last following car of an extra train will display an "X" target by day, a white light at night. At the rear, all cars will display a red flag by day and a red light at night. The absence of a signal marker or light on a car means to the opposing car DANGER, STOP & INVESTIGATE.

120: A motorman finding a red fusee burning in track or runs over one torpedo will stop car at once and investigate

120: A motorman finding a red fusee burning in track or runs over one torpedo will stop car at once and conductor will go ahead to investigate. If safe to proceed beyond fusee, run under absolute control to the nearest point where dispatcher can be called and request orders. A motorman finding a green fusee burning in track or runs over two torpedoes will bring car under immediate control and run for one-half mile at that speed. If no obstruction is met, motorman can bring his car up to speed to the nearest point where dispatcher can be called and request orders.

122: Arc headlights must be carefully centered and marker lamps must be kept burning brightly. Each high speed interurban car must also carry one red and one white hand lantern, and at night same must be kept lit and on the rear platform.

123: For all crossings outside of city, the whistle must be sounded at whistle posts and gong rung continuously until rear of car is clear of crossing.

129: A train must not leave its initial station on any division, or a junction, or pass from double to single track without orders, and until it has been ascertained that all trains due have arrived or left. Train must not start until proper signal is given.

INTERURBANS

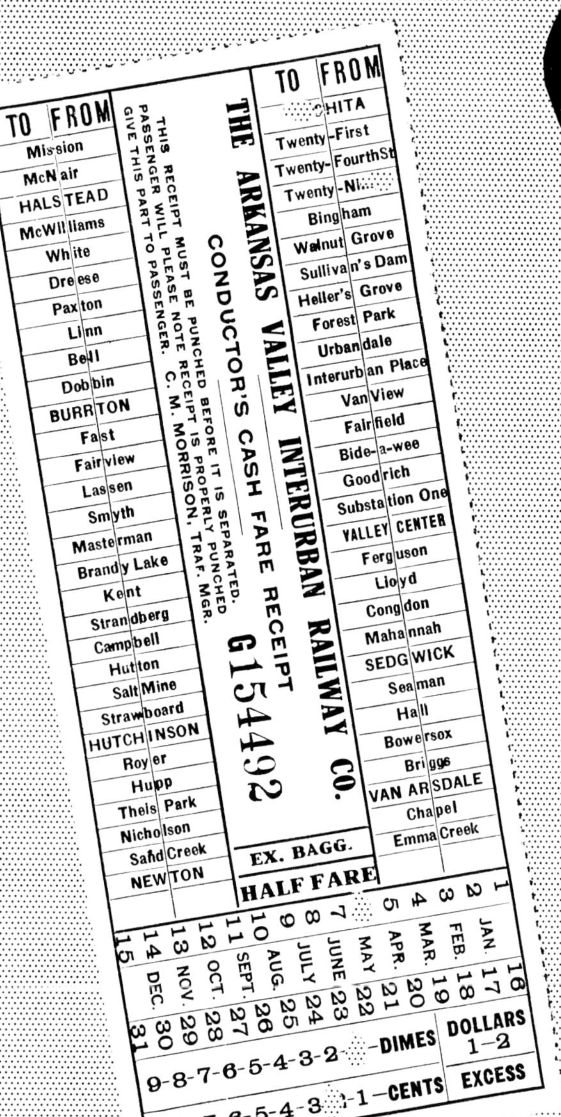

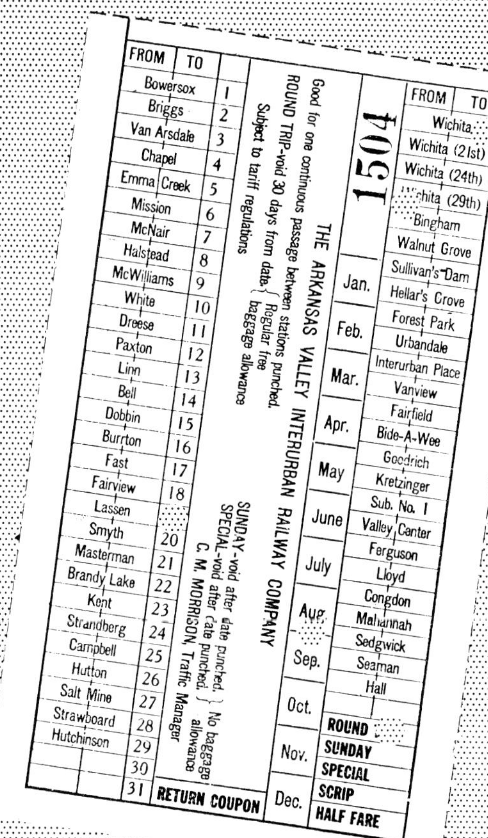

Round Trip Fare to Hutchinson

Wichita	$1.75	Newton	$1.21
Valley Center	1.35	Halstead	.85
Sedgwick	1.26	Burrton	.53

For further information phone our ticket Agent.

Arkansas Valley Interurban Railway Company

"THE ELECTRIC WAY"

Employes' Time Table No. 2

(Cancels Employes' Time Table No. 1)

Main Line and Newton Division

Effective Sunday, July 28, 1918
(5:00 A. M.)

This Time Table is for the government and information of Employes only, and the Company reserves the right to vary therefrom as circumstances may require. Employes will read the rules and study the table carefully.

R. G. KIRWIN, Chief Train Despatcher

A. MARTIN, Train Despatcher

GEO. THEIS, Jr., President   CHAS. H. SMYTH, Gen. Mgr.

Issued by

CHAS. A. STANLEY, Superintendent
Wichita, Kansas

Rules

RULE 1—Standard time clocks will be found in the stations at Wichita, Hutchinson and Newton.

RULE 2—Conductors must register their trains in train register at Wichita, Hutchinson and Newton on departure from or arrival at terminals. They will be required to show exact time of departure and arrival and such other information as required by register.

RULE 3—The classification of trains will be:

Passenger Trains (limited) First Class.
Passenger Trains (local) First Class.
Freight Trains Second Class.
Work Trains Third Class.

RULE 4—All trains of inferior class will clear superior class trains five (5) minutes at Sidings. First class trains when meeting at Switches, train heading into siding will take switch. No first class trains will be permitted to cross over switch points and back into siding, without specific orders from Despatcher.

RULE 5—Limited trains will carry baggage and light express matter between Wichita and Hutchinson ONLY.

RULE 6—Limited trains will stop to take on or discharge passengers at depot only at Valley Center, Sedgwick, Van Arsdale, Halstead and Burrton. At Wichita will stop at depot, Murdock and Twenty-first street and at Hutchinson at depot and Avenue A and Main street and at Second and Main streets Hutchinson in bound only.

RULE 7—Local trains will stop to take on or discharge passengers at points designated as stations and stops as per list of stations furnished employees.

RULE 8—Time shown herein in **bold face type** indicates meeting point.

The small numerals shown in table above the time of certain trains indicates the train which is to meet train for which time is shown at such station.

RULE 9—First class trains will not be required to handle shipments of milk and cream unless otherwise ordered. Such shipments are to be handled on third class trains.

RULE 10—All trains will reduce speed and be under control when approaching the following crossings and must not exceed speed of three miles per hour while crossing in

Wichita—Second street, Third street, Central avenue

Murdock avenue, Ninth street, Thirteenth street and Eighteenth street.

Hutchinson—Walnut street, Sherman and A and Main streets.

RULE 11 — Employees will be required to sign receipt for "Employees Time Table" when delivered to them. Old or defaced time table must be surrendered before new time table will be issued.

Trainmen are required to have in their possession "Employees Time Table" while in the performance of their duty.

CHAS. A. STANLEY, Superintendent.

Wichita, Kansas.

WICHITA-HUTCHINSON=Main Line

Main Line — Trains 29 to 1 (westbound)

STATIONS AND SIDINGS (Mls Wichita / Hutchinson)	29	27	25	23	21	19	17	15	13	203	11	9	7	5	201	3	1
RUN NUMBERS	L-7	L-6	L-9	L-8	X-2	L-7	L-6	D-4	D-3	F-2	D-2	D-1	D-4	D-3	F-1	D-2	D-1
A.M./P.M.	P.M.	P.M.	P.M.	P.M.	P.M.	P.M.	P.M.	P.M.	P.M.	P.M.	Noon	A.M.	A.M.	A.M.	A.M.	A.M.	A.M.
	Local Daily	Local Daily	Local Daily	Local Daily	Local Daily	Local Daily	Limited Daily	Local Daily	Local Daily	Frt Local Daily Ex.Sun.	Limited Daily	Local Daily	Local Daily	Local Daily	Frt Local Daily	Limited Daily	Local Daily
Double Track — WICHITA (0 / 52.3)	11.30	9.20	8.00	6.40	6.10	5.20	4.00	2.40	1.20	12.10	12.00	10.40	9.20	8.00	6.50	6.40	5.30
Double Track — WICHITA, 21st & Mkt. Sts. (2.6 / 49.7)	11.43	9.33	8.13	6.53	6.23	5.33	4.12	2.53	1.33	12.25	12.12	10.53	9.33	8.13	7.05	6.52	5.42
Single Track, 3 Cars — WICHITA, 24th & Main Sts. (3.4 / 48.9)	1.45	9.35	8.15	6.55	6.27	5.35	4.13	2.55	1.35	12.30	12.13	10.55	9.35	8.15	7.10	6.53	5.43
WALNUT GROVE (5.1 / 47.2)	11.49	9.40	8.20	7.00	6.31	5.40	4.17	3.00	1.40	12.42	12.17	11.00	9.40	8.20	7.18	6.57	5.47
10 Cars — FOREST PARK (6.4 / 45.9)	11.54	9.44	8.24	7.04	6.35	5.44	4.20	3.04	1.44	12.47	12.20	11.04	9.44	8.24	7.26	7.00	5.51
5 Cars — INTERURBAN PLACE (7.3 / 45.)	11.58	9.48	8.28	7.08	6.38	5.48	4.23	3.07	1.48	12.52	12.23	11.07	9.48	8.28	7.30	7.03	5.55
2 Cars — St.L. & S.F.Ry CROSSING (11.0 / 41.3)	12.02	9.56	8.36	7.16	6.44	5.56	4.28	3.16	1.56	1.00	12.28	11.16	9.56	8.36	7.38	7.08	6.02
Wye, 5 Cars — VALLEY CENTER (11.1 / 41.2)	12.03	9.57	8.37	7.17	6.45	5.57	4.29	3.17	1.57	1.02/1.11	12.29	11.17	9.57	8.37	7.39	7.09	6.03
3 Cars — FERGUSON (12.8 / 39.5)	12.08	10.02	8.42	7.22		6.02	4.32	3.22	2.02	1.16	12.32	11.22	10.02	8.42	7.43	7.12	6.08
3 Cars — CONGDON (15. / 37.3)	12.12	10.07	8.47	7.27		6.07	4.35	3.27	2.07	1.22	12.35	11.27	10.07	8.47	7.53	7.15	6.12
2 Cars — SEDGWICK (17.6 / 34.7)	12.17	10.12	8.52	7.32		6.12	4.40	3.32	2.12	1.28	12.40	11.32	10.12	8.52	7.58	7.20	6.17
7 Cars — STOC KYARDS (18.2 / 34.1)	12.19	10.14	8.54	7.34		6.14	4.41	3.34	2.14	1.30	12.41	11.34	10.14	8.54	8.07	7.21	6.19
5 Cars — HALL (20.3 / 32.)	12.24	10.19	8.59	7.39		6.19	4.45	3.39	2.19	1.36	12.45	11.39	10.19	8.59	8.14	7.25	6.24
Wye, 4 Cars — VAN ARSDALE (23.3 / 29.)	12.30	10.25	9.05	7.45		6.25	4.50	3.45	2.25	1.45/2.42	12.50	11.45	10.25	9.05	8.20	7.30	6.30
MISSION (25.8 / 26.5)	12.35	10.31	9.11	7.51		6.31	4.55	3.51	2.31	2.50	12.55	11.51	10.31	9.11	8.28	7.35	6.36
Wye, 5 Cars — HALSTEAD (28.3 / 24.)	12.40	10.37	9.17	7.57		6.37	5.00	3.57	2.37	2.57	1.00	11.57	10.37	9.17	8.40/8.53	7.40	6.42
3 Cars — ARMSTRONG (33.3 / 19.)	12.49	10.49	9.29	8.09		6.49	5.09	4.09	2.49	3.16	1.09	12.09	10.49	9.29	9.05	7.49	6.53
1 Car — BURRTON (37.7 / 14.6)	12.58	10.59	9.39	8.19		6.59	5.18	4.19	2.59	3.35	1.18	12.19	10.59	9.39	9.15	7.58	7.02
3 Cars — SIDING No. 1 (40.5 / 11.8)	1.02	11.05	9.45	8.25		7.05	5.22	4.27	3.06	3.42	1.22	12.27	11.05	9.45	9.20	8.02	7.06
3 Cars — COOPER (44.7 / 7.6)	1.10	11.15	9.55	8.35		7.15	5.30	4.37	3.16	3.55	1.30	12.37	11.15	9.55	9.30	8.10	7.16
2 Cars — STRAWBOARD (49.0 / 3.3)	1.15	11.20	10.00	8.40		7.20	5.35	4.40	3.21	4.00	1.35	12.40	11.20	10.00	9.42	8.15	7.25
CITY TRACKS (50.0 / 2.3)	1.20	11.25	10.05	8.45		7.25	5.40	4.45	3.25	4.10	1.40	12.45	11.25	10.05	9.47	8.20	7.30
HUTCHINSON (52.3 / 0)	1.30	11.35	10.15	8.55		7.35	5.50	4.55	3.35	4.20	1.50	12.55	11.35	10.15	10.00	8.30	7.40
A.M./P.M.	A.M.	P.M.	P.M.	P.M.	P.M.	P.M.	P.M.	P.M.	P.M.	P.M.	P.M.	A.M.	A.M.	A.M.	A.M.	A.M.	A.M.
TRAIN NUMBERS	29	27	25	23	21	19	17	15	13	203	11	9	7	5	201	3	1
RUN NUMBERS	L-9	L-8	L-9	L-8	X-2	L-7	L-6	D-4	D-3	F-2	D-2	D-1	D-4	D-3	F-1	D-2	D-1

Main Line — Trains 2 to 30 (eastbound)

STATIONS AND SIDINGS (Mls Hutchinson / Wichita)	2	4	6	202	8	10	12	14	204	16	18	20	22	24	26	28	30
RUN NUMBERS	X-1	D-3	D-4	F-2	D-1	D-2	D-3	D-4	F-1	D-1	D-2	L-8	L-9	L-6	L-7	L-4	L-7
A.M./P.M.	A.M.	A.M.	A.M.	A.M.	A.M.	A.M.	P.M.	P.M.	P.M.	P.M.	P.M.	P.M.	P.M.	P.M.	P.M.	P.M.	P.M.
	Local Daily	Local Daily	Limited Daily	Local Daily Frt.	Local Daily	Local Daily	Local Daily	Limited Daily	Frt Local Daily Ex.Sun.	Local Daily	Local Daily	Limited Daily	Local Daily	Local Daily	Local Daily	Local Daily	Local Daily
WICHITA (52.3 / 0)	6.45	7.42	8.20	9.55	10.10	11.30	12.50	1.40	4.00	3.30	4.50	5.40	7.30	8.50	10.10	11.30	1.30
WICHITA, 21st & Mkt. Sts. (49.7 / 2.6)	6.32	7.30	8.08	9.38	9.57	11.17	12.37	1.28	3.47	3.17	4.37	5.28	7.17	8.37	9.57	11.17	1.18
WICHITA, 24th & Main Sts. (48.9 / 3.4)	6.30	7.28	8.07	9.30	9.55	11.15	12.35	1.27	3.45	3.15	4.35	5.27	7.15	8.35	9.55	11.15	1.16
WALNUT GROVE (47.2 / 5.1)	6.25	7.23	8.03	9.25	9.50	11.10	12.30	1.23	3.40	3.10	4.30	5.23	7.10	8.30	9.50	11.10	1.13
FOREST PARK (45.9 / 6.4)	6.21	7.18	7.59	9.20	9.45	11.05	12.26	1.19	3.35	3.05	4.26	5.19	7.05	8.25	9.45	11.05	1.09
INTERURBAN PLACE (45. / 7.3)	6.18	7.15	7.57	9.15	9.42	11.02	12.22	1.17	3.30	3.02	4.22	5.17	7.02	8.22	9.42	11.02	1.06
St.L. & S.F.Ry CROSSING (41.3 / 11.0)	6.11	7.00	7.52	9.07	9.34	10.54	12.14	1.12	3.22	2.54	4.14	5.12	6.54	8.14	9.34	10.54	12.59
VALLEY CENTER (41.2 / 11.1)	6.10	6.58	7.51	9.05/9.00	9.33	10.53	12.13	1.11	3.20/3.12	2.53	4.13	5.11	6.53	8.13	9.33	10.53	12.58
FERGUSON (39.5 / 12.8)		6.53	7.48	8.53	9.28	10.48	12.08	1.08	3.08	2.48	4.08	5.08	6.48	8.08	9.28	10.48	12.53
CONGDON (37.3 / 15.)		6.48	7.45	8.42	9.23	10.43	12.03	1.05	3.05	2.43	4.03	5.05	6.43	8.03	9.23	10.43	12.48
SEDGWICK (34.7 / 17.6)		6.43	7.40	8.35	9.18	10.38	11.58	1.00	2.56	2.38	3.58	5.00	6.38	7.58	9.18	10.38	12.43
STOC KYARDS (34.1 / 18.2)		6.41	7.39	8.32	9.16	10.36	11.56	12.59	2.54	2.36	3.56	4.59	6.36	7.56	9.16	10.36	12.41
HALL (32. / 20.3)		6.36	7.35	8.26	9.11	10.31	11.51	12.55	2.48	2.31	3.51	4.55	6.31	7.51	9.11	10.31	12.36
VAN ARSDALE (29. / 23.3)		6.30	7.30	8.20	9.05	10.25	11.45	12.50	2.42/1.45	2.25	3.45	4.50	6.25	7.45	9.05	10.25	12.30
MISSION (26.5 / 25.8)		6.25	7.25	8.12	8.59	10.19	11.39	12.45	1.38	2.19	3.39	4.45	6.19	7.39	8.59	10.19	12.24
HALSTEAD (24. / 28.3)		6.20	7.20	8.05/7.55	8.53	10.13	11.33	12.40	1.30/1.20	2.13	3.33	4.40	6.13	7.33	8.53	10.13	12.18
ARMSTRONG (19. / 33.3)		6.11	7.11	7.42	8.41	10.01	11.21	12.31	1.04	2.01	3.21	4.31	6.01	7.21	8.41	10.01	12.06
BURRTON (14.6 / 37.7)		6.03	7.03	7.30	8.31	9.51	11.11	12.23	12.52	1.51	3.11	4.23	5.51	7.11	831	9.51	11.56
SIDING No. 1 (11.8 / 40.5)		6.00	7.00	7.26	8.25	9.45	11.05	12.19	12.47	1.45	3.06	4.19	5.45	7.05	8.25	9.45	11.50
COOPER (7.6 / 44.7)		5.50	6.50	7.10	8.15	9.35	10.55	12.09	12.28	1.35	3.00	4.09	5.35	6.55	8.15	9.35	11.40
STRAWBOARD (3.3 / 49.0)		5.45	6.45	7.03	8.10	9.30	10.50	12.04	12.21	1.30	2.50	4.05	5.30	6.50	8.10	9.30	11.35
CITY TRACKS (2.3 / 50.0)		5.40	6.40	6.55	8.05	9.25	10.45	12.00	12.15	1.25	2.45	4.00	5.25	6.45	8.05	9.25	11.30
HUTCHINSON (0 / 52.3)		5.30	6.30	6.40	7.55	9.15	10.35	11.50	12.00	1.15	2.35	3.50	5.15	6.35	7.55	9.15	11.20
A.M./P.M.	A.M.	A.M.	A.M.	A.M.	A.M.	A.M.	A.M.	A.M.	Noon	P.M.	P.M.	P.M.	P.M.	P.M.	P.M.	P.M.	P.M.
TRAIN NUMBERS	2	4	6	202	8	10	12	14	204	16	18	20	22	24	26	28	30
RUN NUMBERS	X-1	D-3	D-4	F-2	D-1	D-2	D-3	D-4	F-1	D-1	D-2	L-8	L-9	L-6	L-7	L-8	L-9

Note 1 { L-8 and L-6 Change at VanArsdale at 10.25 P. M. / L-7 and L-9 Change at VanArsdale at 12.30 A. M. }

Note 2 { D-1 Relieved by L-6 at 10.30 A. M. / D-2 Relieved by L-7 at 11.40 A. M. / D-3 Relieved by L-8 at 10.30 A. M. / D-4 Relieved by L-9 at 11.35 A. M. } One Day Each Week — Wednesday

NEWTON DIVISION

Trains 129 to 101

STATIONS AND SIDINGS (Mls from Van Arsdale)	129	127	125	123	119	117	115	113	203/204	111	109	107	105	103	101
RUN NUMBERS	L-10	L-10	L-10	L-10	L-10	L-10	L-10	D-5	F-1-2	D-5	D-5	D-5	D-5	D-5	D-5
A.M./P.M.	P.M.	P.M.	P.M.	P.M.	P.M.	P.M.	P.M.	P.M.	P.M.	P.M.	A.M.	A.M.	A.M.	A.M.	A.M.
	Local Daily	Local Daily	Local Daily	Local Daily	Local Daily	Local Daily	Local Daily	Local Daily	Frt Local Daily Ex.Sun.	Local Daily	Local Daily	Local Daily	Local Daily	Local Daily	Local Daily
VAN ARSDALE (0)	12.30	10.25	9.05	7.45	6.25	4.50	3.45	2.25	1.45	12.50	11.45	10.25	9.05	7.30	6.30
THEIS PARK (3.2)	12.37	10.32	9.12	7.52	6.32	4.57	3.52	2.32	1.53	12.57	11.52	10.32	9.12	7.37	6.37
NEWTON (6.0)	12.45	10.40	9.20	8.00	6.40	5.05	4.00	2.40	2.00	1.05	12.00	10.40	9.20	7.45	6.45
A.M./P.M.	A.M.	P.M.	P.M.	P.M.	P.M.	P.M.	P.M.	P.M.	P.M.	P.M.	Noon	A.M.	A.M.	A.M.	A.M.
TRAIN NUMBERS	129	127	125	123	119	117	115	113	203/204	111	109	107	105	103	101
RUN NUMBERS	L-10	L-10	L-10	L-10	L-10	L-10	L-10	D-5	F-1-2	D-5	D-5	D-5	D-5	D-5	D-5

Trains 104 to 130

STATIONS AND SIDINGS (Mls from Newton)	104	106	108	110	112	114	203/204	116	118	120	122	124	126	128	130
RUN NUMBERS	D-5	D-5	D-5	D-5	D-5	D-5	F-1-2	D-5	L-10	L-10	L-10	L-10	L-10	L-10	L-10
A.M./P.M.	A.M.	A.M.	A.M.	A.M.	A.M.	P.M.	P.M.	P.M.	P.M.	P.M.	P.M.	P.M.	P.M.	P.M.	P.M.
	Local Daily	Local Daily	Local Daily	Local Daily	Local Daily	Local Daily	Frt Local Daily Ex.Sun.	Local Daily	Local Daily	Local Daily	Local Daily	Local Daily	Local Daily	Local Daily	Local Daily
VAN ARSDALE (6.0)	6.30	7.25	9.00	10.20	11.40	12.45	2.42	2.20	3.40	4.45	6.20	7.40	9.00	10.20	12.30
THEIS PARK (2.8)	6.20	7.18	8.53	10.13	11.33	12.38	2.28	2.13	3.33	4.38	6.13	7.33	8.52	10.13	12.23
NEWTON (.0)	6.10	7.10	8.45	10.05	11.25	12.30	2.20	2.05	3.25	4.30	6.05	7.25	8.45	10.05	12.15
A.M./P.M.	A.M.	A.M.	A.M.	A.M.	A.M.	P.M.	P.M.	P.M.	P.M.	P.M.	P.M.	P.M.	P.M.	P.M.	P.M.
TRAIN NUMBERS	104	106	108	110	112	114	203/204	116	118	120	122	124	126	128	130
RUN NUMBERS	D-5	D-5	D-5	D-5	D-5	D-5	F-1-2	D-5	L-10	L-10	L-10	L-10	L-10	L-10	L-10

130: A following section must not leave stations and stops under two minutes after preceding section has left and unless some form of block signal is used, the trains must keep at least 2,500 feet apart, except when closing up at stations, crossings and meeting sidings. Must keep behind leader at least one block on city streets.

132: Regular cars will invariably have right of way over extras unless dispatcher gives contrary orders. Extras must clear all other cars at sidings and turnouts by five minutes.

133: Work trains will always be considered as extras and as such must yield right as above indicated.

140: If a train should part while in motion trainmen must, if possible, prevent damage to detached portions. The front section must be kept in motion until the detached portion is stopped.

145: For movements not provided for by Time Table, train orders will be issued by authority and over the signature of the Train Dispatcher. They must contain neither information nor instructions not essential to such movements. They must be brief and clear; in the prescribed forms when applicable; and without erasure, alterations or interlines.

146: Cars on time are not required to be reported to dispatcher unless they fail to meet opposing cars at meeting points, get blockaded or disabled on the road, or are stopped by a train order signal.

147: Whenever a car becomes three minutes late after passing a time point on time the dispatcher must be called for orders at the first switch unless contrary orders have been previously received from him.

148: When cars make a meeting point by dispatcher's orders, the motorman of first car arriving must report his arrival, also the arrival of opposing cars.

149: If at any time a motorman is in doubt of the position of his first opposing car he must stop at first plug box and ask for orders from dispatcher and have conductor protect rear end of cars. Do not stop on curve for this purpose.

150: When reporting to Dispatcher, motorman must follow this rule and give first: Direction in which car is headed; second: Train or Car number, according to rule by bulletin; third: Point at which he is calling. As follows: Northbound Train 43; Kirkwood; and at the same time write that information on order blank.

151: An order received from Dispatcher must be written on order blank as it is received, and motorman will sign his initials to order; Conductor will then read order back to Dispatcher; if correct the Dispatcher will say "Complete." Conductor will then sign his initials to order. If Dispatcher orders car held, leave telephone connected, and when final order is given write it as directed above. If telephone becomes disabled, Dispatcher may give written orders through motormen, or verbal orders through any channel which he may see fit to use, and such orders are to be obeyed.

152: If Dispatcher wishes to give an order through a station agent, latter will be ordered to set order board against car.

158: When a train is named in a Train Order all its sections are included unless particular sections are specified.

159: Agents will promptly record and report to the Dispatcher the time of departure of all trains and the direction of extra trains. They will record the time of arrival of all trains and report it when so directed. They must have the proper appliances for hand signaling for immediate use if required.

162: Failure of Telephone. If Dispatcher cannot be called, after several attempts, examine plug and cord carefully for any trouble which motorman may repair. If he is satisfied that the fault rests with the telephone line, after waiting ten minutes,

proceed slowly with great caution, the conductor going ahead at blind curves with a flag or lantern at least ten poles ahead of car, and motorman sounding whistle frequently on curves. Under these conditions, durfogs or stormy weather, run very slowly sounding whistle, and stopping frequently to listen for approaching car. Always take the SAFE SIDE, however, and stand still rather than endanger life and property.

165: Train Dispatchers report to and recieve their instructions from the Superintendent. They will issue telephone orders for the movement of trains; see that they are transmitted and recorded in the manner prescribed in the rules; keep a record showing the time of arrival and departure of trains at all open telephone offices. Such record to be carefully filed for subsequent reference. They must use great care in sending orders, and not transmit an order faster than receiving motorman or agent can take and plainly write it. They will anticipate the necessity for orders as far as possible and have them ready for trains; compel a prompt performance of duty on the part of trainmen, with a view to preventing delay.

166: Conductors and motormen receive their instructions from the Superintendent. They will also comply with the instructions of the Dispatcher.

170: Conductors of passenger trains will pass entirely through their train after leaving each station where their train has stopped, for the purpose of collecting the tickets and fares; and where stops are made at long intervals, they shall frequently pass through to look after the comfort of their passengers.

174: Toilets must be locked while cars are on the streets of any city or town through which they may pass.

175: When taking a car having a hot water heater, see that water in expansion tank is at proper height, that ash pan is properly cleaned, that fire is in good condition, and a sufficient amount of coal is on car to run at least one round trip. Put on only a small amount of coal at each firing; by so doing smoke and gas are prevented.

176: Motormen are required to observe the position of all switches and must know that such switches are right before passing over them.

181: Motormen will exercise caution and good judgment in moving and coupling cars, and in stopping and starting trains, and must avoid all unnecessary jerking, so as to prevent disturbance to passengers or injury to persons or property.

182: If a car carrying follower signals does not receive acknowledgement of same from opposing car, the stop signal must be given by motorman of leading car, his car brought to an immediate stop and motorman of opposing car called to account for his failure to signal.

185: On city streets within the limits on bulletin board, high speed interurban cars must never be operated at a higher speed than that allowed by the full series position of controller handle.

186. The last stop at the end of each run must be made with the hand brakes. If car is stopped at any time for more than the regular passenger stop, set the hand brake and release the air. When leaving car in barn, set hand brake and release the air.

187: When leaving car in barn, shut off the cutout switch and open reservoir drain cocks. During periods of cold weather, test drain cocks several times during the run and drain off any water which may have accumulated.

And in this manner AVI operated its cars for many years. But time was running out for the big interurban cars, just as it did on countless other interurban systems, far and near. As each succeeding year brought fewer patrons, AVI cut back service, added freight trailers, and cut corners whenever and wherever possible. But there finally came The Day:

<u>DECLINE & END</u>: When AVI was young, its passenger business accounted for 95% of the road's annual earnings. As good roads and better automobiles came, the ratio changed until by 1938 passenger revenues were but 5% of the total. The story is told well in the Wichita "Beacon" on July 31, 1938:

"A future of even greater service looms for the AVI. Expansion plans of this widely known and popular electric line were revealed by Robert B. Campbell, trustee and general manager, in the company's recent application for permission to discontinue its passenger business.

"It was the AVI's planning-ahead policy that caused it to apply for permission from the Kansas Corporation Commission to become an exclusively freight-carrying railway. The hearing on the application was held at the Allis Hotel a few days ago and a favorable decision was given, effective at such time as AVI desires to inaugurate its strictly freight business.

"The changing modes of passenger transportation---and nothing else---were responsible for the discontinuance of the AVI passenger business and the resolution to build an exclusive and more extended freight business. Service was the underlying cause.

"Only a few years ago, the AVI electric trains carried nearly a million passengers annually and proceeds from passenger service amounted to a half million dollars a year. This was more than 90% of the company's revenue at that time. Now, conditions are reversed.

"Mail business, under government contract, has been reduced by establishment of other train routes which web Wichita's territory.

"If the passenger business would only support itself, Campbell told the Commission, AVI would gladly maintain it as a service to its patrons. It was made plain that the company could not afford to maintain the service at an expense to itself. And it is not fair to expect it to pay rent and overhead on stations which only a few passengers use each week.

"The AVI head said the gradual downtrend of passenger business was due entirely to the rapid perfection and general use of automobile and bus service. Contributing to AVI passenger business a few years ago, theater parties were planned to Wichita from nearby points and shoppers used the line in large numbers. Persons employed in small towns rode to Wichita, Newton and Hutchinson daily. A special attraction, circus or carnival would crowd the AVI cars to capacity. Not so today.

"The family motor car has been the competitor of the interurban. The Valley Center station, ten miles from Wichita, has been rendered completely useless and will be discontinued.

"With money saved through this action, Mr. Campbell pointed out, the AVI company will be able to give freight service greater than ever before."

And so, on August 31, 1938, AVI's last passenger cars rolled to a stop. As one of the last riders put it: "Mary Agnes, Paul and I rode the last passenger car out of Wichita at 8:00 PM today, went to Van Arsdale and returned on last car into Wichita at 9:40 PM. Car #8 to Van Arsdale, #3 into Wichita, Motorman Dan Marks, Conductor Homer Cummings. Great fun, and many happy memories."

AVI's passenger motors, except for #12, were mothballed. The 12 was rebuilt at once into an express car and ran for several more years. When AVI became Arkansas Valley Railway and diesels took over, a couple of old passenger motors once again ran on their own power on the farewell day to electricity.

In November 1937 the ICC refused to approve a plan or any plan of reorganization, stating it was apparent the probable future earnings of AVI would be insufficient to assure payment of operating expenses.

TAPPING THE FIELD
. . . By R. E. Reifschneider

IMPRESSIONS OF THE A.V.I.: One who was familiar with the AVI only in its last few years may not have gained the true perspective of someone who knew the line throughout its existence. Here was a true interurban in the classic tradition, a fast electric railway with frequent service between the important cities in its territory.

Perhaps in those happier days when the train and the rail were the bulwark of local transportation rather than the auto and the road, there may have been many local passengers between Wichita and Newton and intermediate towns, but it is hard to envision more than city to city riders over the vast flat prairies from Van Arsdale through Halstead and Burrton to Hutchinson. Perhaps people did wander in to the interurban from ranch houses hidden behind the rises in the prairie, and flag the cars where dirt trails intersected the tracks, but in later years there were few stops except at the well built stations in the towns; a local could make about the same time as a limited if the motorman felt like putting it on the brass.

The AVI had good track, with few curves or grades and made good speed. Here is one of the few interurban lines where a modern high speed car like those of the Cincinnati & Lake Erie could have made 85 to 90 miles per hour for many miles on end and possibly cut one-fifth or more off the running time.

The AVI Station in Wichita was one of the best anywhere---a station which many a larger company might well have envied. And one last word should be said: in an area where interurbans were uncommon, the AVI was well and favorably known. It was an institution which almost everyone knew well and which most of them thought would go on forever. It is hard to recall an area where the interurban occupied so prominent a place in the lives of its citizens.

I once wrote a poem inspired by memories of the AVI; this poem was published in Railroad Magazine and with that magazine's kind permission, I close with this tribute:

Ghosts of the limited ride the rails
Across the Kansas prairie trails,
In memory fond of the days gone by
Of the folks who rode the AVI.

Van Arsdale sub lies stark and gaunt,
Naught left of power there to haunt
The sparking wires to Valley Center
Where next the energy would enter
The speeding big red cars to send
To Wichita at journey's end.

In aptitude there is no phrase
The curtain of the past to raise
To bring once more within our view
The interurban that we knew.
If only I with stroke of pen
Could bring it back to us again!

In fantasy without delay
The interurban's on its way;
The prairies echo to the chime
Of whistle as in olden time---
A glorious chance for you and I
Once more to ride the AVI.

⬤

After Arkansas Valley Railway took over AVI and dieselized it, the timecard reproduced at extreme right was in effect. The clipping at the right is from the Wichita "Evening Eagle," Friday, July 24, 1942 and shows diesel 92 as it tied up in Wichita for the last time.

⬤

⬤ "In fantasy without delay the interurban's on its way---" and here's No. 5 near Wichita.

Above is a scene in the Wichita Station yard in 1937; cars from left to right are 202, 602 and 3. Broadview Hotel in background.   (RH)

LAST AVR TRAIN REACHES WICHITA

PICTURED ABOVE is the last train of the Arkansas Valley Railroad as it reached Wichita Thursday at 11 p. m. The Interstate commerce commission has allowed the road, formerly known as the Arkansas Valley Interurban, to discontinue service. Contract for dismantling the road will be let soon. For years the line operated between Wichita and Hutchinson, first with electric traction but later with Deisel locomotives.

FREIGHT TRAIN SCHEDULE
DAILY EXCEPT SUNDAY

FROM WICHITA

Lv. Wichita	7:00 AM	12:01 PM	6:00 PM
Ar. Valley Center	7:32 AM	12:34 PM	6:32 PM
Ar. Sedgwick	7:49 AM	12:49 PM	6:48 PM
Ar. Van Arsdale	8:05 AM	1:15 PM	7:05 PM
Ar. Newton		1:35 PM	
Ar. Halstead	8:20 AM	1:29 PM	7:20 PM
Ar. Burrton	8:45 AM	1:51 PM	7:45 PM
Ar. Hutchinson	9:45 AM	2:45 PM	8:45 PM

FROM HUTCHINSON

Lv. Hutchinson	12:01 PM	5:15 PM	9:00 PM
Ar. Burrton	12:37 PM	5:54 PM	9:39 PM
Ar. Halstead	12:57 PM	6:14 PM	9:59 PM
Ar. Van Arsdale	1:15 PM	6:30 PM	10:15 PM
Ar. Newton	1:35 PM		
Ar. Sedgwick	2:21 PM	6:48 PM	10:31 PM
Ar. Valley Center	2:33 PM	6:58 PM	10:42 PM
Ar. Wichita	3:20 PM	7:45 PM	11:30 PM

FROM NEWTON

Lv. Newton	1:45 PM	
Ar. Van Arsdale	2:05 PM	
Ar. Halstead	7:20 PM	Extra service to and from Newton on carloads.
Ar. Burrton	7:45 PM	
Ar. Hutchinson	8:45 PM	
Ar. Sedgwick	2:21 PM	
Ar. Valley Center	2:33 PM	
Ar. Wichita	3:20 PM	

Closing time 30 minutes prior to departure of train.

Free pick up and delivery service at Wichita, Hutchinson and Newton.

Direct connections and through rates with rail and truck lines at Wichita, Hutchinson and Newton, giving expedited service to and from all points.

Wichita	Hutchinson	Newton
Phone 4-3541	Phone 5502	Phone 77

ARKANSAS VALLEY RAILWAY, Inc.

Quick, Convenient and Dependable Service

Chapter 6

Freight Operations

AVI originally was a passenger-hauling interurban line, but as the auto came more and more into its own (as hard surfaced all-weather roads crept relentlessly across the face of Kansas) the company had to take a good, long look at its future. Perhaps it was an agonizing reappraisal (which we hear much about these days), but it resulted in AVI's reorienting its policies and facilities in favor of freight hauling. Freight revenues surpassed those of passenger in the late Twenties and thereafter, but AVI was actually in the freight business in a minor way from the day it first opened.

Early freight carrying took the form of less-than-carload business capable of being transported in the baggage compartments of passenger cars. Probably the chief item of freight at the beginning was cream; cars paused at wayside shelters, loaded cream cans and took them into Wichita, where the creameries picked them up by wagon. The De Coursey Creamery was probably the largest user of AVI-hauled cream. Bakeries of the three principal cities sent out countless boxes of fresh bread on the speedy and frequent interurban cars; the Sutorious Bakery (Pan Dandy Bread) of Newton, the Tip Top Bakery of Wichita and the Betts Bakery of Hutchinson were all patrons. AVI liked this business and made preparations to garner more of it. Freight trailers were purchased, two big express motors to haul them came in 1916 and freight rooms were set up at principal stations. Passenger cars were often seen hauling one or two freight cars, sometimes to the dismay of city residents who were unused to the sight of such trains passing down their quiet streets. To build up its freight business, AVI rebuilt an old work car into a locomotive in 1923; this was capable of hauling up to twelve freight cars of any type or size at a respectable rate of speed.

AVI went after the cattle hauling business by building loading chutes at Sedgwick, Van Arsdale, Halstead and near Burrton. The bulk of the beef cattle hauled by AVI went to packing houses in Wichita and Hutchinson. The Cudahy and Dold packing houses of Wichita were heavy shippers, realizing full well that the interurban's three-freights-per-day to Hutchinson enabled their products to reach southwest Kansas and southeast Colorado at the maximum speed. In 1930, AVI bought two refrigerator cars, largely to handle this business; Cudahy and Dold meats were rushed to Hutchinson where they were reloaded in Rock Island reefers for shipment as far as Liberal.

AVI attracted the wheat business by constructing tall corrugated iron-covered grain elevators at Sedgwick and near Van Arsdale. Wheat from these elevators went to both Wichita and Hutchinson flour mills.

Here is a typical AVI freight train of the mid-Thirties: Express motor 203 is seen hauling refrigerator cars 3000 and 3001 at speed near Valley Center. (ES)

Hutchinson's salt industry and the Carey, Barton and Morton evaporative plants became regular shippers on AVI, especially for shipments to Wichita and beyond. In 1923 a new salt mine (448 down to a vein of rock salt 400 feet thick) was opened by Carey adjacent to the AVI main line in East Hutchinson; in order to reach his plant, Carey obtained trackage rights over a mile of AVI track to get his salt to his Hutchinson & Northern Railway. Production from this mine rose enormously and eventually AVI reaped the benefit of greater salt shipments to the southeast.

Two miles west of Burrton was the Olson Oil Company which was served by tank cars on AVI rails for many years. The Compressed Steel Company of Wichita collected cars of scrap metal by using AVI. AVI hauled a good number of sand cars; a large commercial sand company was located on the east bank of the Little Arkansas River midway between Wichita and Valley Center.

In 1929 AVI's freight business looked so promising that a new steel locomotive was purchased from General Electric. This motor could haul up to thirty cars---but around the corner was the Depression and this big motor was never utilized by AVI to its full degree of productivity.

In later years, AVI was used by wholesale firms and large retain chains for the quick distribution of their goods. Among such patrons were the Wichita Furniture Company, the Goodyear and Goodrich companies, Kress and Woolworth chains, and McKesson & Robbins wholesale drug chain. Woolworth workers in Hutchinson recall drays from the AVI Station bringing them crated wooden boxes of imported Chinese and Japanese pottery; this continued until the beginning of World War II.

However important the carload business was, the less-than-carload business was even more so. In this field, AVI could give the steam roads more than enough competition. As a result, most of the competing steam

roads were willing to institute interchange
agreements with the interurban (Santa Fe
never would!); physical connections were
made at the following points: Wichita
(Missouri Pacific and Midland Valley),
Valley Center (Frisco), Burrton (Frisco),
and Hutchinson (Rock Island, Hutchinson &
Northern).

AVI interurbans also carried the mail.
Mail pouches were carried in the baggage
compartments of the interurban cars to and
from all post offices on the system. AVI's
many and frequent schedules gave its area a
very fine mail service.

However attractive freight hauling might
have appeared to be, AVI's power problem was
an obstacle to the most complete realization
of the line's potential. For instance, the
big GE locomotive with its four 135 hp motors
strained the capacity of AVI's power system
badly. A new 500 MCM feeder was installed
from Valley Center Substation to Wichita KG&E
to handle the heavy power demand of the sand
trains. This, of course, did nothing for the
remainder of the line which was designed for
light, frequent passenger service rather than
heavy intermittent freight service. Not only
did the substations and line need to be aug-
mented, but KG&E had long since become dis-
illusioned with its once fair haired customer
now no longer able to pay its power bill on
time. AVI was that unattractive thing: a
customer with high intermittent loads and a
small total demand. To increase substation
capacity would have meant higher costs per
kilowatt hour. AVI, like any power user,
paid a certain high monthly charge to KG&E
to cover that company's cost of maintaining
the necessary generating and transmission
capacity to take care of any need which might
arise; after that, power could be bought at
bargain rates. So little was being used in
later years that, by 1934, power costs had
risen from less than .005¢ per kilowatt hour
to .013¢. To increase substation capacity
simply to start a freight train a few times
daily (and thereby boost the cost of power
again) was unthinkable.

Studies indicated that, were AVI to put
in diesel prime movers at its substations,
savings of as much as 75% might be realized
but this would not have solved the problem
of inadequate capacity for heavy freights.
With passenger cars the company had a rule
that whenever a power outage occurred, even
numbered cars were to start as soon as the
power came on again and odd numbered cars
were to start a minute later. With entire
trains starting, it was impossible to do
this. Substation voltage had been boosted
to 625 volts, which was all the machines
could put out. Bypass switches at the two
circuit breakers separating the KG&E and R
KP&L from AVI's three substations were kept
closed so that the central stations could
help out. Even so, a line drop of 300 volts
(a 50% power loss) was not uncommon when
starting between substations with a long
train---yet motormen had to be cautioned to
use extra care when feeding up near the subs
to avoid blowing the breakers in the hopped
up (625 v.) substations.

In 1934 serious consideration was given
to dieselizing both passenger and freight
service. One idea was to install diesel
prime movers on board the best cars (12,
202, 203 and 602). Another was to purchase
new diesel-electric locomotives for freight
hauling and a couple of light gas-mechanical
cars for the remaining passenger business.
Studies were made by supplier companies such
as Westinghouse, Kalamazoo and Plymouth and
it was determined that an auual return of
20% on an investment of $76,960 would have
been possible. But bankrupt AVI had no way
to raise such a sum; it couldn't even pay
its taxes, power bills or joint trackage
rentals.

However, as a result of the surveys made
in 1934 we have a good picture of the way
AVI's freight business appeared that year:
"We are hauling approximately 100 to 150 ton
trains Wichita to Hutchinson with motors 202
or 203 at an average speed of around 25 mph,
and approximately 350 tons Wichita to Hutchinson with the same motors at around 15 mph"
(letter from Superintendent Ailee Martin to
Messrs. Campbell and Vallance, 10-12-34).
At that time, each motor express car was

● Rain or shine, snow or heat---AVI moved the freight. Here we see express
motor 202 and trailer at speed in a snow storm about 1938. 202 and its
near-twin 203 hauled most of AVI's freight trains at fairly high speeds.

● Here we see locomotive 602, AVI's best, hard at work north of Wichita. (ES)

making one round trip daily between Wichita and Hutchinson hauling from 2 to 12 cars, the maximum train weighing 400 tons; time each way was usually four hours for the 115.2 miles. Capacity was determined by the Santa Fe overpass near Newton; this hard pull was a 1½% grade which occupied a half mile of track and which was the same in either direction. On each trip, about 15 stops of four minutes each were made per train each way. 202 & 203 made these trips daily except Sundays and holidays. The two locomotives, 601 & 602, were used in extra service, handling carload lots; several times a month it was necessary to handle a full tonnage train of approximately 800 tons.

Freight was also handled in trailers behind regular passenger cars. In 1934 cars 2 and 12 handled one refrigerator car and LCL on the night trip at 6:30, as well as passenger, express and LCL service at 10:30, 1:00 and 3:30; 110 minutes was required to perform this run from Wichita to Hutchinson.

<u>Typical Freight Run:</u> Superintendent Martin made the following report on a run he accompanied; following is a verbatim report of his memorandum:

"Memorandum of my observations of the movement of Local Train Motor 202, leaving Wichita at 12:10 PM, arriving Hutchinson at 3:15 PM, September 27, 1934, showing LCL tonnage handled at intermediate points, car loads picked up and set out, time used at each point switching, also arriving and leaving time at each point:

```
Left Wichita 12:10 PM pulling trailer 257
Ar. Frisco Connection Valley Center 12:42
            (Picked up one load)
Lv. Frisco Connection Valley Center 12:46
Ar. Valley Center    (no tonnage in)12:47
Lv.    "      "      ("   "  out)    12:48
Ar. Sedgwick   (195 lbs. in)          1:04
Lv.    "       (no tonnage out)       1:06
Ar. Van Arsdale (set out 257)         1:19
Lv.   "     "   (no ton. in or out)   1:24
Ar. Mission  (met Extra 203 east)     1:29
Lv.    "     (met Train #26)          1:46
Ar. Halstead  (4,860 lbs. in)         1:54
Lv.    "      (let #26 around)        2:07
         (Weak power, Burrows to Bell)
Ar. Burr ton   (404 lbs. in)          2:34
Lv.   "        (no tonnage out)       2:36
      (Weak power, Brandy Lake to Strandberg)
Ar. Carey Lake (set out one car to    3:02
Lv.   "     "    H&N engine)          3:06
Ar. Hutchinson Yards                  3:13
Spotted to freight dock               3:15.
```

"Total time Wichita to Hutchinson, 3 hrs. 5 minutes. Unloaded 5,459 lbs. freight; handled one car load Valley Center to Carey Lake and one trailer Wichita to Van Arsdale (where it was set out for Newton). Made 32 stops including switching stops.

"Only one delay from Wichita to Hutchinson, that being 18 minutes at Mission. This deducted from the 3 hrs. 5 mins. total means all of above work handling LCL tonnage, car load, switching, etc., was done in 2 hrs. 47 minutes. During this period they were either unloading freight or train was actually in motion.

3:18 – Two Rock Island employees and two transfer men began sorting shipment of meat.
3:27 – Check clerk arrived in car.
3:30 – One more R.I. employee began work.
3:30 – Began loading freight on two transfer trucks from car.

●

3:50 – One truck left with freight.
3:52 – Discovered one short and one over on meat shipment. Check clerk went to call Wichita. Other employees left car and went in freight house.
3:55 – At this time about half of tonnage was unloaded, balance still in car. There was a total of approximately 11,000 lbs. of freight in this car for Hutchinson and points beyond of which less than 6,000 lbs. had been

unloaded by four R.I. employees and two transfer men during forty minutes. This seems rather slow; however, I noticed considerable time was spent determining correct names on packages and this was caused by illegible marking. I inspected a number of these myself and it was very difficult to read the writing.

"I do not want to comment on this particular movement too much until further investigations are made. I understand the poor marking of packages has been handled a number of times with the shippers but so far have been unable to get much results. I also understand the steam roads experience the same trouble and there doesn't seem to be much we can do about it unless we refuse the shipments and that, of course, we cannot afford to do."

By 1938, passenger business constituted but 5% of AVI's total revenues and regretfully Trustee Robert B. Campbell asked and received permission to give up passenger service and concentrate on freight hauling. At that time AVI announced plans to expand its freight facilities considerably to be able to serve better the rich Arkansas River Valley.

On July 31, 1938, the Wichita "Beacon" said: "A future of even greater service looms for the AVI. It is the aim of the AVI management, in discontinuing its passenger business, to devote itself wholly to the further expansion of its freight business. In this way it hopes to meet the needs of the area it serves by affording patrons a fast, dependable and economical general transportation service over its electrified lines.

"Both equipment and service schedules are to be of the highest class with a manpower that is highly trained and experienced. One of the praiseworthy results of the company's change to an all-freight line will be the employment of all but four of the men losing their jobs through discontinuation of passenger service."

"Interurban Bob" Campbell and his AVI cohorts went to work with a will to make the freight-only policy pay off. The stations at Valley Center and at Hutchinson were closed, saving more than $5,000 annually; this money was spent remodeling passenger motor 12 into an express car. World War II began within a year and Wichita, the air capital of the southwest, spawned numerous defense plants——none of which were built on or near AVI lines. Everyone prospered but AVI——and the freight-only policy seemed to be barely holding its own. Then came the sale of AVI to the H. E. Salzberg Company of New York, a combined scrap-metal and operating company.

● Freight for Newton was usually set out from the Wichita-Hutchinson through train at Van Arsdale and there picked up by passenger motor 5, one of two double-ended passenger cars on AVI. Here 5 and 256 are at Newton. (ES)

Above, express motor 12 at Rock Island Station, Hutchinson.

Below, locomotive 601 hauls the Valley Center oil train. (EV)

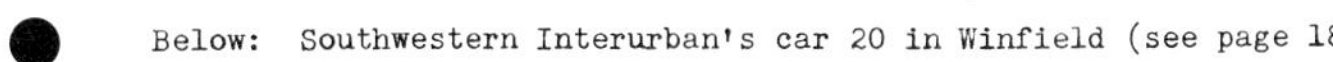

Above: AVI 202 at Wichita Station about 1936; note two headlights. (ES)   ●   Below: Southwestern Interurban's car 20 in Winfield (see page 18).

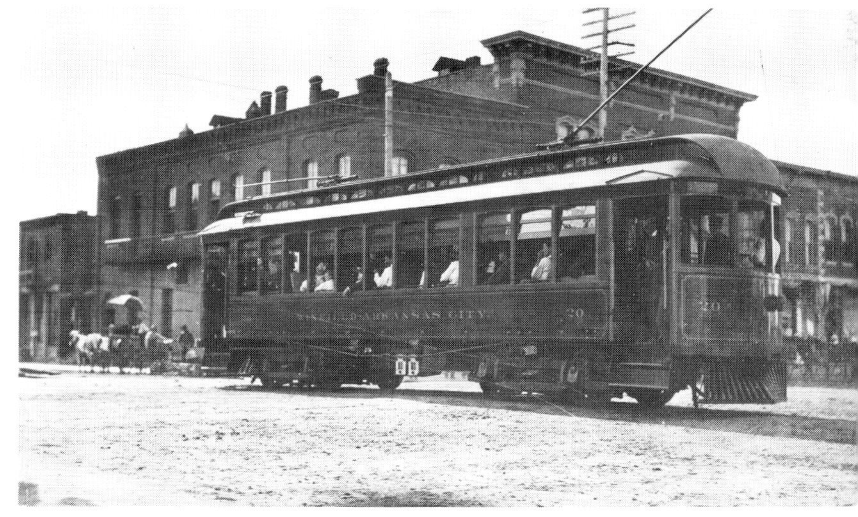

Above: 1942, Hutchinson; car 202 demotorized.   (MDI)

Below: Late 1921 view of Wichita Station yard; cars
202, II 2 and 11. Station at extreme right.

BALLAST (Continued from P. 19)

urgently needed much more so than was the case with a rock-ballasted railroad. The crushed rock gave firm support in any weather while permitting proper drainage. Unballasted track, especially in the midwest, is a labor-intensive thing and there are fewer days when weather permits the track crews to work it.

The immediate area lacked deposits of rock which could be crushed and screened, thus ballast had to be brought from some distance, or some material of a local nature had to be found. The Frisco line, for instance, served lead mines in eastern Kansas and used chat ballast at Wichita. The AVI owned a sizeable deposit of gravel at Walnut Grove and used this for ballast. Screened and graded gravel was a good ballast material BUT the AVI used it in "bank run", or as-it-came-from-the-gravel-bank condition. Thus it was about 25% gravel (of varying size) and the rest was sand, including some very fine grains. Sand could be worked, wet, much better than mud and it had the same supporting power wet as dry, but it was readily displaced in either condition by vibration or the intermittant loads imposed by passing cars. Also dust, of which there was a super-abundance during the early Thirties, filled up the voids between the sand particles. Before long the bank-run gravel ballast was little better than the natural soil. In fact, it was hard to tell the two apart except for the large polished sandstones scattered through the gravel ballast.

Floyd Harrison mentioned some use of burnt clay ballast, which came from he knew not where, on the Frisco, and AVI's last major rehabilitation of track, through Halstead, used some crushed rock, but, for the most part, AVI ballast was just ordinary soil.

A RARE SIGHT ON THE A V I, crushed rock ballast was dumped to the rail head on Main St., Halstead, in 1932.
-Eugene Sabin

Immediately after bankruptcy the track crews were reduced to three men each and the tie replacement program was suspended. The track declined from that point on and became quite rough.

There were various things the track crews could do when it was too wet to work on the track, including burning the plants along the right-of-way. If this was not done a smoking passenger or a hot bubble of copper from a dewirement might set the grass on fire, at a later date, when it was dry. A self-propelled Fairmont weed burner was used in later years.

During the Depression some residents north of Wichita began keeping goats, apparently in a effort to make ends meet. They pastured these on the AVI right-of-way and the goats sometimes refused to yield right-of-way to the trains. This was yet another reason for burning off the right-of-way.

The most important track crew job, however, was to maintain track alignment and on the poorly ballasted AVI their work was never done.

MIDWESTERN CAR TRACKS: Typical streetcar track on small to moderate-sized midwestern city streets, was light T-rail laid of often-untreated wood crossties, frequently without ballast and virtually never with tie plates. Over this was a layer of sand and on top of that paving brick. (A specially-shaped brick was used inboard of each rail to provide flange clearance.) Most routine track maintenance involved removal of the pavement. Joints were the most pressing problem and were, usually once a year, jacked up. Arc welders running on the trolley current were used to built up the battered rail ends.

The era of extensive street paving, between 1900 and 1920, saw most thoroughfares important enough to have car tracks paved. The ties lasted only so long and by the Thirties car tracks were wearing out all over the area.

With the coming of the Depression and resultant layoffs of track crews, rail deteriorated so rapidly that abandonment was an almost certain outgrowth of deferred maintenance. The joints would slowly batter down into the decaying ties, forcing up the paving until bricks erupted at each joint. Where single truck cars were used the ride resembled that of a moving teeter totter.

under such circumstances it might be necessary to rig the fenders to give more than standard clearance to save their being torn away.

(Continued on Page 20)

BRIDGES AND VIADUCTS: The AVI had extremely level terrain. The ruling grade was 1½% over the man-made Santa Fe overpass. This was a ruling grade in theory only. There was no interchange north of the overpass and a maximum of 325 feet of storage track for cars at Newton. The overpass was a steel girder structure on concrete abutments. Clearance of 23 feet above the Santa Fe grade was maintained; 6,000 cubic yards of fill were used in the approaches.

Pile trestles were used at first but were regarded as temporary. In 1916 a concrete bridge was built across Sand Creek between Sedgwick and Hall siding. The AVI always crossed Sand Creek, on Fifth, in Newton, on a pile bridge south of the Fifth St. wagon bridge. At the time this was built trolley cars were generally required to use a separate roadway on bridges because it was thought hazardous for a trolley car to frighten a horse on a bridge.

HIGH WATER. The Arkansas Valley Interurban bridge across the little Arkansas River at Halstead stood up to a July, 1929 flood, which brought water to the tops of the ties. Note the double overhead in these views, and also the natural soil ballast. - both Eugene Sabin, Ailee Martin Coll.

Two years later, in 1913, when the AVI crossed Sand Creek on the way to Bethel College, this prohibition had apparently been rescinded because there it used the wagon bridge. (See middle photo P. 16) By 1919, earth-filled arch bridges had been constructed over East and West Emma creeks and across the Little Arkansas River at Halstead. The bridge at Halstead withstood the 1929 flood and is still standing (1977).

The AVI was well on its way to having all concrete bridges and culverts when the relocation into Wichita was made. The involved five new pile trestles. About 40 feet of the trestle, south of Seneca, washed out in May of 1942 giving the final reason for abandonment. (Four of these pile trestles are shown on the map on page 28, the other was across the Little Arkansas at Olive and Mascot and the Perry pr/w.) IN ALL, 1,335 feet of pile trestles were constructed at Wichita to accomplish the relocation.

SPEED AND POWER

How fast did the AVI cars go? How much would they pull? Trolley car performance is a set of complex, interacting variables. The only sure way to tell how fast a car will go is to time it over a given distance. In AVI-1 and this was easy to do. There was a road on each section line and they were exactly a mile apart. Of course timing could be accomplished by counting poles or milepost distance; the cars lacked speedometers.

So far as we can learn there was never an official speed record for the AVI but we have many "unofficial" reports. Motorman John Hargit told Eugene Sabin that he once ran (2nd)#2 with 100 passengers on board at 70 MPH between Hutchinson and Burrton, in limited service. The car had just been shopped and had all new wheels. Sabin also states that both (2nd)#2 and #12 ran in the 60-65 MPH range while he was on board.

In discussing the first Halstead run the *Eagle*, of Dec. 20, 1911, says that at times the first car traveled between 40 and 43 MPH going to Halstead and attained between 50 and 55 MPH returning. The entire return trip of 28½ miles was accomplished in one hour and 12 minutes.

POWER SUPPLY: (Continued from P. 27)

The extra feeder from Burrton substation to the Brandy Lake breaker may have been installed when the capacity at Hutchinson was reduced to 300 KVA. In later years all the circuit breakers between substations were by-passed so that the substations and central stations could help each other move increasingly long freights. The voltage at the substations was also raised to 625 volts at that time.

To give an insight into the amount of power required to move AVI trains, here are figures for the 1932-33 era: Power consumption for the first five months of 1933 was 577,377 kilowatt hours, or 115,000 kilowatt hours per month. The consumption from March 1, 1932 to February 28, 1933, was 1,585,000, or 132,000 monthly. Of this, KG&E supplied 85% on the average, with the remainder coming from Hutchinson (Kansas Power & Light Corporation). For this power, AVI paid KG&E 1.695¢ per KW hour and paid KP&L 2.395¢ per KW hour. AVI didn't get full value for its money expended for AC as its substations had motor generator sets and the power was measured at the high side, losses were appreciable---not only at the substation but on the line as well. These losses ran about as follows: transformer loss, 2%, line loss, 6%, light running loss, 4%, loss in motor generator sets, 15%---a total loss of 27%! At this time AVI was operating three passenger round trips per day which account for only about one-third of the total power consumed; the exact figures: for passenger service, 478,000 KW hours, for freight service, 962,000 KW hours.

When asked the balancing speed of cars (2nd)#2 and #12 Elmer Vallance, AVI's final general manager, unhesitatingly replied 45 MPH. For cars 3-10 the answer was the same. He said that, for #202 and #203 the figure was 35 MPH.

By "balancing" speed he meant the standard speed at which cars are rated. This is the speed the car will finally attain, on level track, without wind, at rated voltage and with a load of 150 pounds for each seated passenger. At this speed the propelling force of the motors is just equal to the retarding factors of friction, motor windage, back electromotive force of the motors and air resistance to the car. The propelling and retarding forces are in balance. If the car goes down a grade this augments the motor force so that it goes faster but, as it does so, all of the retarding forces increase so there is a new balancing speed (a higher one) than is the case on the level. Differences in line voltage and wind direction, as well as velocity and (of course) the condition of the car, all influence speed. As a motorman, the author has been surprised by the spirited performance of cars under favorable conditions and also knows well the lethargic behavior with drastically reduced voltage.

Well, how powerful were they? Traction motor manufacturers were the opposites of auto and motorcycle makers in that they customarily understated the capabilities of their product. Typical horsepower ratings for automobiles tell how much the engine will put out, at the maximum, under standard conditions. The traction motor ratings tell what the motor will produce, continuously, under *any* probable conditions.

As to horsepower, traction historian Felix Reifschneider says, "(The subject of) motor ratings is a complicated problem. I believe the method of rating changed at one time. The original motors were quite open but when GE and Westinghouse got in the act, they were totally enclosed. The GE #800 motor rating was a completed one based on drawbar pull under certain conditions. However, motor ratings were soon based on temperature rise. The temperature rise was the allowable rise depending on where the reading was taken. Generally 100° C was the maximum rise adopted. There is a nominal rating (which is, I believe, a one-hour rating) and a continuous rating. When the desired temperature rise in measured, horsepower is calculated by the ampere and voltage readings at that time.

"It is well known that a railway motor will develop three or four times its horsepower rating for a short period of time, such, for instance, as when the car is starting up..."

This, of course, is drastically different from using a dynamometer, or prony brake, and then quoting the highest possible figure, as is done, by an auto maker. The engine will rarely attain that exact speed and throttle setting in a traffic situation.

Rail cars use much less power, per ton mile, than do highway vehicles. Compared to an internal combustion engine, the free-turning resistance of an electric motor is very small and, when no power is being applied, the car will coast, like an automobile in neutral. Steel wheels running on steel rails offer far less rolling resistance than rubber tires on pavement. A rail car can attain a dangerous speed, from an unpowered start, on a grade on which an automobile would neither start of itself nor keeping rolling, if pushed.

Thus #12, with 320 rated, continuous, horsepower, and weighing 40 tons, could pull two trailers, weighing 70 more tons, and still run from Wichita to Hutchinson in one hour and 45 minutes, make all of its intermediate stops, and stay on time!

The AVI cars were a varied lot, but they had some things in common. None had field shunts. All, except perhaps #602, had series-parallel control. All but #201 and #602 had type K controllers. The passenger cars had a 2.5:1 gear ratio or a ratio very close to that. #202, #203 and #601 had a 3.625:1 ratio. All of these had 34" wheels.

#602 was in a class by itself. AVI's newest and most modern unit; designed and built by the world's foremost builders of electric locomotives; it had a gear ratio of 4:1 and, when new, had 36" wheels. It *may* have later received 34" wheels. It had a master controller which controlled a bank of contactors. These contactors carried the motor current. It probably had at least 14 points and may have had series/series-parallel control with three running points. It was reportedly very slow but with excellent adhesion.

It weighed 186 pounds per horsepower, compared to #601's 226-lb. per HP and, with 36" wheels, went 25.6 MPH at 1,000 motor RPM. With 34" wheels the speed was 24.9 MPH. #601, at the same motor speed, went 28 MPH. Because of the greater horsepower one would expect #602, when running light, to about equal the speed of #601 running light, but this was not the case. All reports indicate otherwise. We asked Eugene Sabin about this and he replied:

"Something has to be wrong of the specifications indicate that #601 and #602 were equally slow - they definitely were *not*. #601, as the roster states, could handle 10-12 cars (500 tons) at 25-35 MPH. #602 was a drag engine and I would guess that it could only attain 25-30 MPH, running light. With any kind of heavy train, say 15 or more loaded cars, it moved no faster than 12-15 MPH. Several times I had the opportunity to run #601 pulling two freight trailers and I would estimate it easily attained 35-40 MPH. It was a good riding engine, although a little slippery when switching loads around the yards. #602 was a rough-riding loco (above 20 MPH) but could handle heavy switching duties without undue slipping."

The better adhesion of #602 is explained by its superior control. Not only did #601 have a type K controller but it also had a relay which cut off power when the motorman rotated the handle back toward the first point. This reduced contactor arcing in the controller but it also meant that, if the motorman found an axle slipping he could not reduce the power by one or two points. He had to go back to "power off" and feed up from point one. During this delay the train would loose inertia. The alternative would be to apply the brakes slightly but the brakes, in 1929, were not uniform in application. The force was almost never equalized among the axles and it might be first applied to an axle which was not slipping, thereby making the slippage worse. It was not until 1961 that GE produced a locomotive with an automatic and selective braking action applied to a slipping axle.

As to speed, the most plausible explanation seems to be that our gear ratio data is incorrect. Standard, series-wound, traction motors were in universal use on low-speed interurban locomotives of that day. This is an intriguing mystery for one who like conjecture and research but the deadline is here and we still don't know. Perhaps the reader can find out.

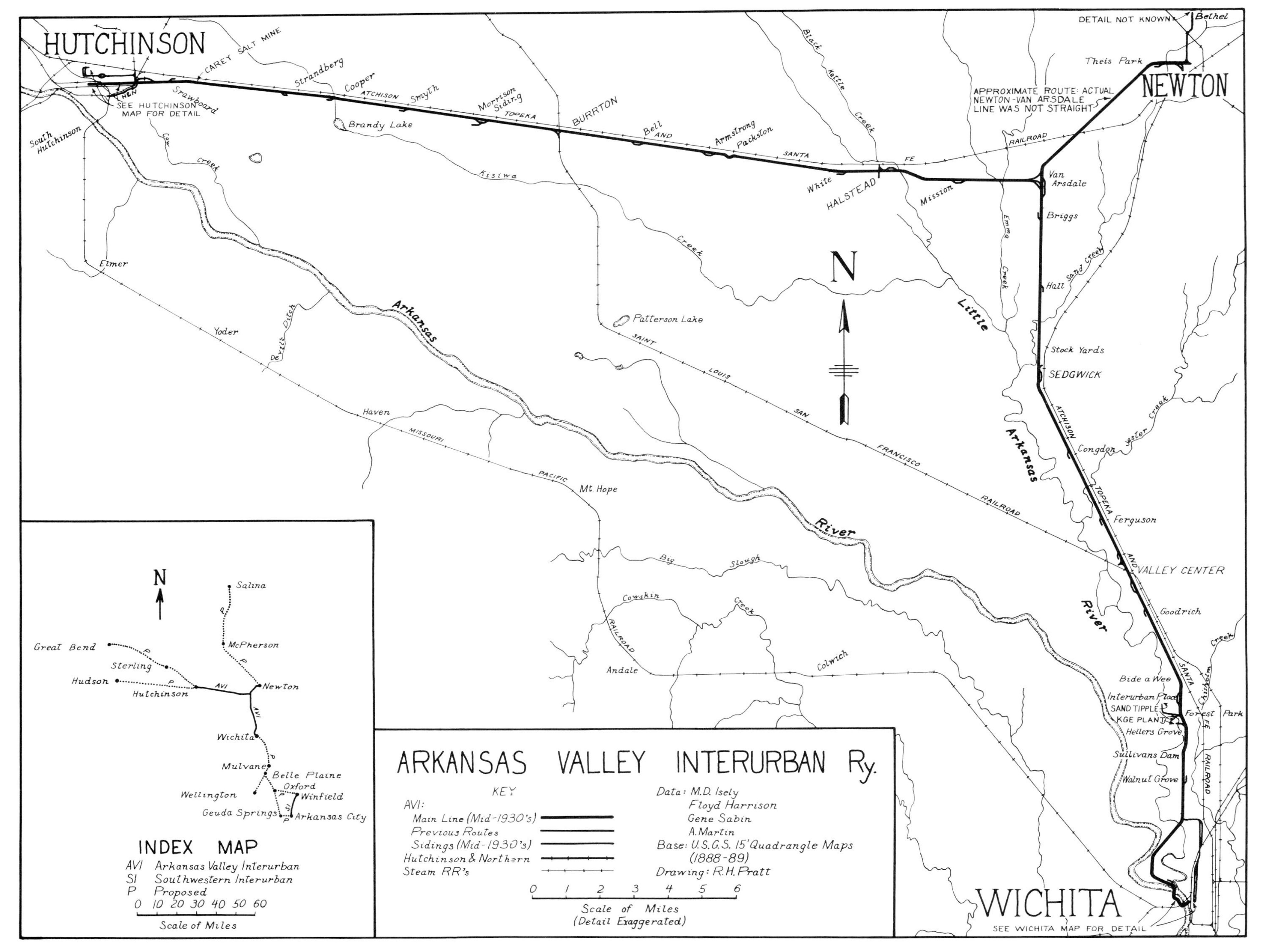

HUTCHINSON
NEWTON
WICHITA
DETAIL NOT KNOWN
Bethel
Theis Park
APPROXIMATE ROUTE: ACTUAL NEWTON-VAN ARSDALE LINE WAS NOT STRAIGHT
CAREY SALT MINE
Strawboard
SEE HUTCHINSON MAP FOR DETAIL
South Hutchinson
Strandberg
Cooper
ATCHISON
Smyth
Morrison
Siding
TOPEKA
BURRTON
Bell
AND
Armstrong
Packston
SANTA
FE
RAILROAD
Van Arsdale
Briggs
Hall
Sand Creek
Brandy Lake
Kisiwa
White
HALSTEAD
Mission
Emma
Creek
Little
Creek
Black
Kettle
Creek
Jester Creek
Stock Yards
SEDGWICK
ATCHISON
Congdon
TOPEKA
Ferguson
AND
VALLEY CENTER
Goodrich
Arkansas
River
Elmer
Yoder
Derth Ditch
Cox
Creek
Arkansas
Patterson Lake
SAINT
LOUIS
SAN
FRANCISCO
RAILROAD
Haven
MISSOURI
PACIFIC
Mt. Hope
River
Big
Slough
Cowskin
Creek
RAILROAD
Andale
Colwich
N
Bide a Wee
Interurban Place
SAND TIPPLE
KGE PLANT
Hellers Grove
Forest Park
SANTA FE
RAILROAD
Sullivans Dam
Walnut Grove
SEE WICHITA MAP FOR DETAIL
N
Salina
McPherson
Great Bend
Sterling
Hudson
Hutchinson
P
P
AVI
Newton
AVI
Wichita
Mulvane
Belle Plaine
Oxford
Winfield
Wellington
Geuda Springs
P
P
Arkansas City
INDEX MAP
AVI Arkansas Valley Interurban
SI Southwestern Interurban
P Proposed
0 10 20 30 40 50 60
Scale of Miles
ARKANSAS VALLEY INTERURBAN Ry.
KEY
AVI:
Main Line (Mid-1930's)
Previous Routes
Sidings (Mid-1930's)
Hutchinson & Northern
Steam RR's
Data: M.D. Isely
Floyd Harrison
Gene Sabin
A. Martin
Base: U.S.G.S. 15' Quadrangle Maps
(1888-89)
Drawing: R.H. Pratt
0 1 2 3 4 5 6
Scale of Miles
(Detail Exaggerated)

MORE ABOUT WICHITA (1977 Notes)

WICHITA RELOCATION: AVI cars entered the First & Water station by backing off Main St. onto First and into the station. This awkward movement made possible trailing switch points, with attendant safety from derailment, on the heavily traveled Main St. tracks of the streetcar company but had no other redeeming features. Because of the delay, people began leaving the cars on Main St. and the company began the practice of stopping for them at the near side of First and Main to let them off. This delayed four streetcar lines while the unloading took place. The AVI cars first loitered along after the many city cars with local stops. The city cars then lined up at First and Main behind an AVI car making a stop of long duration.

The AVI cars had only one entrance-exit with steps having high risers, and they had narrow aisles with wide, luxurious seats. Womens' styles of the time tended to restrict movement, so a woman in high heels, hobble skirt and hat with a brim two feet across would have trouble getting her luggage and packages off the car. She might even slowly back down the steps, assisted by the conductor. One can imagine a car, with a standing load, taking five minutes at that stop.

On August 14, 1916, AVI requested a safety zone at First and Water, and the request was granted. But, on October 7, 1917, an *Eagle* article states, "Hardly a day goes by that some complaint is not heard about the way the AVI ties up traffic at First and Main....." Other reports stated that the protracted unloading was an accident hazard. On May 26, 1920, the city, at AVI's request, passed a resolution, not an ordinance, requiring the AVI to back into the station before discharging passengers. Reading between the lines we gather that AVI didn't want to offend, or perhaps couldn't control, its patrons and hoped that a resolution, which presumably wouldn't stand up in court would ease the situation until they could move into their new station.

When the AVI was built Wichita's business center was at about First and Main. However, Douglas Ave., one block south, and Lawrence Ave., two blocks east, were developing rapidly and, by 1920, the center of the business district was nearer Market and Douglas. There was no vacant land near Market and Douglas and increasing street traffic, especially automobiles, delayed the AVI and produced an accident hazard. Thus, once the Hutchinson extension was out of the way, a new route into downtown Wichita was sought.

Downtown Wichita had grown to the edge of the floodplain east of the Arkansas River and then a program began to fill in a part of this land to provide more downtown real estate. The AVI was able to obtain enough reclaimed land for a large, uncrowded, depot.

This was just north of Douglas Ave., .2 of a mile longer and three minutes faster than the old route. Three city streetcar lines, leaving their pile trestle across the river, stopped almost at the curb at the station door. These cars ran right down booming Douglas Ave. past the Union Station with its Santa Fe, Rock Island and Frisco trains. It was just across the river from the Midland Valley station, which also accomodated Orient trains and it was in clear view of the Missouri Pacific station and not much farther from it than the old AVI station.

From 1916 until 1918, nothing was done about the new station due to World War I, but with that over plans were finalized and, on August 30, 1919, the *Eagle* reported that the AVI was actively building south, putting in its first pile trestle at 20th and Mascot.

The AVI originally planned to cross the river at Second St. but the city objected. This would have involved only two pile trestles instead of four. The AVI leased Ackermans Island, with its old wonderland park, from A. E. Nuttle. The city planned to put a park on the south end of the island and arranged, with the AVI, to do so, but then rescinded its action.

The AVI located its shops on the northern part of the island and built a wooden stadium and playing field in the center. The Wichita Railway & Light Co. had a stop with elevated platforms to its pile trestle at the south end of the island and with the AVI transported many to the football and baseball games at the field. Motorists could drive in from Second St. and park north of the stadium.

The new AVI freight station, on Waco, was finished before the passenger facility and passenger trains began stopping there on November 8, 1920; the new owner of the old AVI station wanted to occupy it at the earliest possible time.

THE FREIGHT PICTURE: The Wichita relocation put the AVI into the carload freight business in a bigger way. Before the Hutchinson line it could interchange with only one railroad, the Frisco, at Valley Center. With its new rail connections at Hutchinson and Wichita it was able to attract some bridge traffic as well as local business in the area. It originated very little carload freight; at Wichita it served only the Water Works and, in later years, the Wichita City Shops, but it transferred freight expeditiously between its connections.

It soon had a 50=ton steeple cab motor capable of doing the work of a typical steam switch engine with a weight of 70 tons on drivers. (When a steam switcher was waiting for an assignment it leaked steam and radiated heat; the electric used no power with the trolley down.) The motor had a two or three man crew while the steam engine required four, and the entire AVI was on an hourly rather than a trip-pay basis. Maintenance and servicing of the electric was minimal and it cost less than $15,000. An interurban was well-equipped to compete with the main line railroads for short haul movements, at that time.

■

WICHITA'S CONNECTIONS: Wichita had not been included in the Santa Fe's original plans and the Santa Fe had blocked neutral connections between Wichita and the Rock Island's Golden State Route, at Pratt, by buying the Wichita & Western. In fact, Wichita seems to have forced itself on the Santa Fe, which accepted it with reluctance and accepted its interurban not at all! The AVI's one major competitor among the main line roads was the Santa Fe. But the AVI's connections generally helped the other roads compete with the Santa Fe and they cooperated with the AVI to that end.

At Wichita, the AVI connected, physically, with the Missouri Pacific and, through it, with the Santa Fe, Rock Island and Frisco. It also connected with the Midland Valley which, like the AVI, had 70-pound rail and unballasted track (but the MV also had large track crews and daily, all-steel passenger trains serving Arkansas Valley points such as Tulsa and Ft. Smith.) Through the Midland Valley, the AVI was linked to the Kansas City, Mexico & Orient.

The "Orient" was built by the Stillwell group which had built the Kansas City Southern. It had been projected to run from Kansas City to Acapulco, Mexico, and managed to make it from Wichita to a point south of San Angelo, Texas, where the money ran out; but it served a growing agricultural area.

In the 1970s, Santa Fe operates the ex-Orient line as far as Sonora. The Midland Valley has been torn up (it was absorbed by the Texas & Pacific). In 1920 they were both small, shaky (but useful) railroads and both interchanged business with the AVI.

WICHITA'S NEW FACILITIES: The Wichita buildings the post-World War I depression and the workmanship was excellent. The building trades had been espcially hard hit and there was an abundance of willing, skilled labor at perhaps 60% of the high wages charged during the war.

The shops were 120' x 156', one story, with concrete block walls and wood truss roof, covered with asphalt roofing. They included a paint bay separated from the rest of the building by a concrete block firewall, a separate coil room and a very complete machine shop, with such tooling as a 350-ton press and a wheel lathe. There was space for twelve cars in the shops. Exclusive of equipment, the structures cost $14,000. The Hutchinson & Northern deadheaded its locomotives there for major repairs (see P. 24 and 26).

The new brick and reinforced concrete freight and passenger stations cost $125,000, and $4,700 was spent on kitchen and dining room equipment for the passenger facility. This station had a wood-framed gable roof covered with green tile. The same red tapestry brick used for the exterior comprised the walls of the waiting room with its ceiling height of about 30 feet. Shops occupied the ground floor to the south, flanking the Douglas Ave. entrance. A balcony crossed two sides of the waiting room giving access to company offices, all with outside windows. The interior architectural treatment was novel and pleasing, making uncommon interior use of a master mason's skill.

With all these improvements in service, the AVI felt justified in raising rates. Freight rates now became 15% higher and passenger fares ½¢ per mile more (a 20% increase). This was done during a business downturn (the first American depression called by that name). Wartime prices, especially for wheat, had collapsed. George Theis later said that he expected the excellent service would enable the AVI to hold its own against bus competition. The AVI policy was to be service-oriented rather than price-oriented, yet standing loads were routinely carried even though a seat, if obtainable, was better than the competion could offer. The competition, in later years, was in the form of Fegeol Safety Coaches. These had cross seats, similar to those in summer cars, but with sedan doors at all seats so that they could not carry standees. Also the bus price was less. AVI passenger business declined from the time that the fare was raised. Freight business, however, boomed.

WICHITA CARS TO THE FAIR - SPECIAL MOVES

The HI used to rent Wichita cars to provide extra service to the State Fair and they operated over the AVI. AVI specials even served one fair. Ailee Martin told of how the operation was planned in advance and then, when it was too late to stop the cars, someone wondered if they would clear certain structures on the fairgrounds! They apparently would because they did, to everyone's relief.

Kansas teachers held regional conferences twice each year. The south central region held one at Wichita and the other at Hutchinson. School was out on Thursday and Friday and the students were on their own. On one such occasion, at least one student watched the AVI move the teachers. There must have been about eight cars and half of them pulled trailers. One trailer was a steel coach from the Frisco.

The fall weather was pleasant and the baggage compartment doors were open revealing rows of folding chairs, with no aisle, and a teacher in each seat. The teachers could detrain right at the auditorium on Avenue A and go from there to their hotels after the day's convention.

fering six cylinders in some models while
Autocar built only 49 of its two-cylinder
classics that year.

The AVI had good track and excellent stations. The service was frequent and reliable.
It was swifter than driving but very little
swifter than it had been before; the cars
were luxurious but it was a somewhat dated
luxury. The new shops had modern equipment
but gandy dancers still used hand tools.

1940   All Kansas cities and most towns
were linked by hard-surfaced roads. State and
national programs tied the major highways together in an interconnecting network not unlike the rail net. A motor shovel had one operator as did a patrol grader. Gasoline was
high in quality, low in price and eminently
available.

The auto and the truck were the almost
universal means of local transport. Even the
cheapest cars went more than a mile a minute and, although low in price, were more
reliable and durable than ever. It was hard
to find a new truck with a top speed of less
than 55 MPH.

THE AVI AND ITS COMPETITORS: The AVI ran, as
an interurban,
for 29 years and 11 months. Its only serious
competition came from motor vehicles. Here
we compare the two rivals, at the beginning,
halfway through the AVI's existence, and at
the end.

1910   Kansas roads were built by the counties and each county built roads to its county
seat. There were no through roads and NO road
signs. It was permissable for a farmer to pay
his taxes by maintaining the roads; this he
did without benefit of engineering advice and
with agricultural implements.

An automobile ride was considered a novel
and daring adventure. A few autos could exceed 60 MPH but were priced beyond the reach
of most people. The Model N Ford cost about
$800. Motor trucks generally had solid tires
and speeds ranged from 12 to 20 MPH. An "ad-
vanced" truck of the period was offered by
White Motors; a two-ton, pneumatic-tired model, capable of 30 MPH in overdrive fourth.

It was an era of rough roads and no shock
absorbers, dusty roads without air cleaners,
primitive lubricants without oil filters,
pneumatic tires which might fail abruptly
(even when new). A successful self-starter
was in the realm of science-fiction. Autos,
as such, were highly unreliable and there
were few repairmen outside cities.

The AVI cars were beautiful, modern and
luxurious. They attained speeds of 45 MPH

over a smooth, all-weather roadbed linking
major cities without regard for petty poli-
tical jurisdictions. The cars and all their
related equipment were reliable but, if
something should go wrong, a professional
staff stood ready to make it right.

1925   By this time 18-foot wide brick
paving extended a few miles north and a few
miles west of Wichita and Arkansas Ave. was
paved with concrete north of the city. Paving and road maintenance were labor inten-
sive and expensive. A steam shovel had a
crew of three (engineer, fireman and coal
passer-swamper). The rest of the paving
crew was as fully staffed. A road grader,
coupled to a Holt tractor, also had a three-
man crew. Even so, Hutchinson, Newton and
Wichita were now linked by all-weather sand-
clay roads.

Automobiles were rightly regarded as dangerous but were widely accepted. Reliabili-
ty and durability had increased and almost
any farm boy could make minor repairs and adjustments. More people could afford cars and
a five passenger Model T Ford touring car cost
$290 F.O.B. Detroit. An electric self-starter
was offered as an option. Starters were standard on all other cars.

Hard tired trucks, bearing data plates
which warned that speeds in excess of 20 MPH
voided the user's warrenty, dominated the
roads but several builders produced trucks capable of sustained speeds of 45 MPH. Branhams
reference book shows most truck builders of-

Things were rough during the Depression
and one of the roughest things in Kansas was
the AVI track. The maintenance-of-way department now had a Fairmont weed burner but
there was no money for ties and only a skel-
eton track crew. Passengers placed their
luggage on the many vacant seats so that it
wouldn't bounce out of the overhead racks
onto their heads. One motorman observed
that #602 rode well at speeds below 12 MPH.
Understandably enough, the passenger business had died, quietly, in 1938.

The AVI employes went resolutely about
their business, using the old, worn out
equipment to serve, as best they could, a
diminishing group of shippers. The general public was scarcely aware that the AVI
existed.

CONCLUSION: When the AVI was founded,
interurban rail technology, with 25 years
of dynamic development behind it, was at
its zenith. During the following quarter
of a century the motor vehicle industry
solved its problems as quickly and as well
as the light electric railways had solved
theirs a few decades earlier. Moreover,
the auto and truck offered total area cov-
erage with the convenience of individual
transportation--- all at a price the AVI
couldn't match!

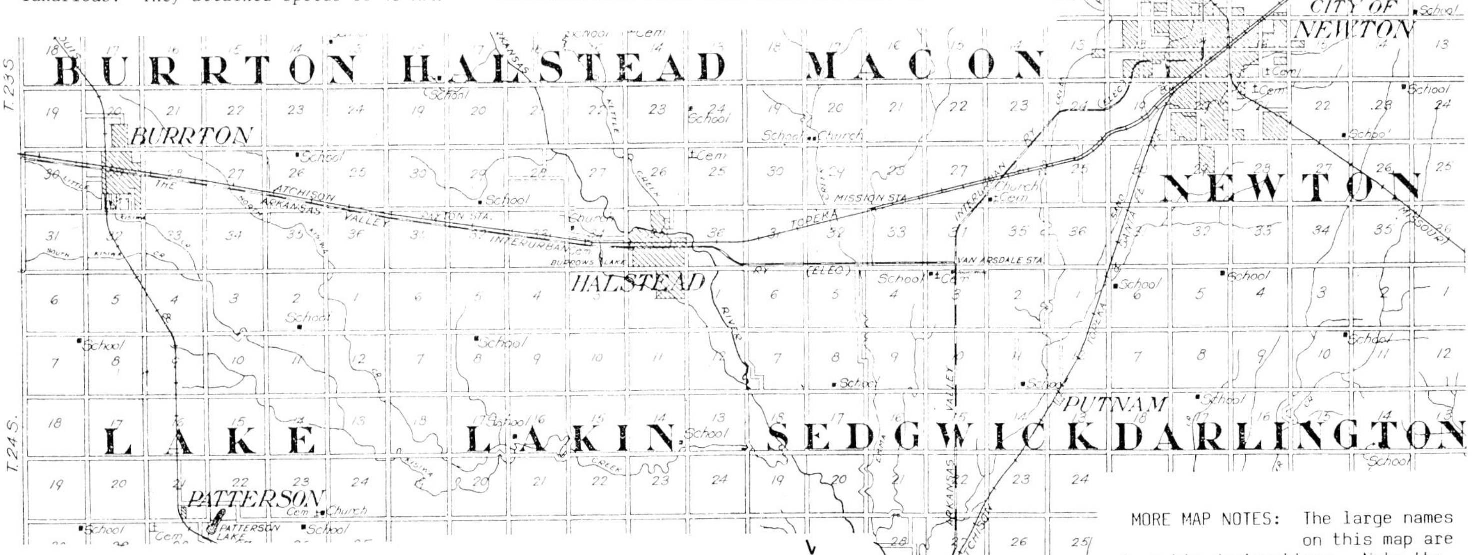

This segment from a recently-discovered 1918 map series supplements the
AVI map on P. 56. It shows more detail of the Newton area entrance.

MORE MAP NOTES: The large names
on this map are
township designations. Note the
country roads laid out one mile
apart.

PATRONS OF THE AVI- Passengers: Passenger business

built the AVI. Freight failed to save it. The line opened on Saturday, November 19, 1910. Both cars were used and a one-hour headway maintained from 10 a.m. to 10 P.M. The trip was described as "scenic" and, perhaps, there was beautiful autumn foliage. Fare to Valley Center was a quarter; to Sullivan's Dam it was a dime. 1.091 were carried on that opening day. From this modest beginning AVI business boomed for nine years. The company undertook to attract riders at every opportunity.

An aviation meet was held near Sullivan's Dam on May 4, 5 and 6, 1911, and Clyde Cessna, who built the first cantilever monoplane and founded Cessna Aircraft, was one of the exhibitors. The AVI built a spur track to accomodate the crowds and, in addition to its three cars, rented all of the local Wichita systems double-truck cars as well as their baseball trailers. This fleet enable the AVI to dispatch four cars from downtown Wichita to the meet every ten minutes. (Santa Fe also ran three special trains.) Sullivan's Dam, was an attraction in its own right, as the water was deep enough for swimming. Many escaped there during the oppressively hot, humid summer months to beat the heat.

The AVI itself developed Walnut Grove as a beach resort. In 1912 the AVI built a bath house with 90 lockers for men and 50 for women. On July 4th, 1913, 3,000 people visited.

The Walnut Grove facilities must have been as overloaded as the cars, judging from an AVI advertisment in the *Eagle* of May 26, 1914, announcing a shuttle service into Walnut Grove Park, connecting with all main line cars after 9 a.m. On Thursday evenings half-hour headways were maintained after 6 P.M. to carry Wichitans to band concerts.

This prosperity, however, was short lived. The new concrete dam, just north of Central, impounded a quiet lake more than a mile long. It was ideal for boating and the water depth, at the Murdock St. boat house, was enough so a 70=foot diving tower was installed. There was no beach but the lake wound its way through Wichita's scenic parks and past beautiful homes. By 1916 Walnut Grove was open for picnics but dark at night. The AVI hoped to lease it to someone who would put in a conventional amusement park; something Wichita never had.

To gain patronage the AVI also subdivided real estate along its route. Those who desired the advantages of semi-rural living combined with a fast, dependable transit line to downtown Wichita could buy one-acre lots at Urbandale, or five-acre lots at Interurban Place.

The research of Dr. Edward N. Tihen into the files of the Wichita *Eagle* gives considerable insight into the rise of AVI's passenger business. The accounts given show certain discrepencies, which may be due to approximate figures being given and to optomistic overstatement by AVI officials. Also, some say "passengers carried", presumably including "deadheads" (non-paying passengers) while others specify paying passengers, or fares. After passenger business peaked there are no accounts for several years. Apparently a declining patronage was no cause for press releases. In later years some mention is made but mostly in connection with a request to abandon passenger service.

--By Oct. 8, 1911, the AVI was carrying 30,000 people a month plus 50 carloads of freight, mostly produce. On Oct. 12, it began hourly passenger service between Wichita and Newton. The first car left Wichita at 6 a.m. and arrived at Newton at 7:30 a.m. Box motor #201 made two trips a day. Fare to Newton was 65¢ but $5 books of tickets reduced this to 52¢.

--In Nov. 1911, 35,000 people rode the AVI and on Dec. 19 the pilot operation into Halstead ran, regular service following on the next day. With completion of the line into both Newton and Halstead business boomed.

---In June, 1912, 41,105 passengers were carried. During July the figure rose to 57,501 and in August AVI collected 61,508 fares. The old settlers picnic, at Halstead, caused 6,340 persons to ride the AVI.

---On Nov. 19, 1912, the AVI was two years old and had carried 751,092 paying passengers to date. When new it had operated two cars over nine miles of its own track plus 3½ miles of WRR&L (the local Wichita streetcar system) track. Now it operated 15 cars over a total of 34¼ miles of track of which more than 30 was its own.

---The length of the average ride increased with the Hutchinson extension and, with it, the average fare. The costs also increased. In Oct., 1916, 70,160 rode and for August, 1917, the total was 73,904.

---A July, 1917, article tells us that the AVI was considering a sleeping car from Hutchinson to Wichita. Thus passengers from points west could avoid changing cars in the middle of the night and arise, after having spent part of the night sleeping, aboard the car, at First and Water.

---We find no further mention of this and, we think, that the idea was hatched in the front office without consultation with the operating department. Such a car would surely have been a standard Pullman from Los Angeles and the sleeping car of that day was very large and very standard. The AVI made six turns on Wichita streetcar tracks with a radius of 40 feet or less. The turn from Market onto the private right-of-way paralleling the MoPac tracks was much less, although it was not a 90° turn. Extensions between the couplers could have kept the corner of the Pullman from colliding with the corner of the AVI car but the Pullman had six wheel trucks. One can imagine such a truck wedging its flanges in the grooved rail at one of the curves and requiring several AVI cars to provide enough weight on drivers to push it off!

---Suppose that the Pullman had made it to First and Main and then gone on the ground. Wichitans would find, by the dawn's early light, a Pullman car, crosswise of the streetcar tracks, in one of the major intersections of the business district; blocking the way of the streetcars pulling out from the barn.

---Apparently this great plan was revealed to the press and only then did the official glowingly bring his idea to Supt. Faulkner who, with firm courtesy, must have said the 1917 equivalent of "No Way!"

---In 1918 the line carried 743,550 passengers and in 1919 there were 826,500. This was the high point in AVI riding. On May 15,

1920, AVI fares were raised from 2½¢ per mile to 3¢ per mile, making them the same as steam road fares. The AVI and Santa Fe mileages were different, however. From Newton to

Wichita via AVI the mileage was 29.3 whereas Santa Fe's route was only 27.2. From Hutchinson to Wichita the AVI traveled 52.3 and the Santa Fe 60.1. Missouri Pacific operated a daily train between Hutchinson and Wichita but it was slow and uncompetitive. About this time Greenleaf Stages linked Wichita, Newton and Hutchinson with about 2¢/mile fares. Greenleaf thus offered some mild competition.

---In May, 1927, the AVI fares rose to 3.6¢ per mile, making the Newton-Wichita AVI rate 99¢ compared to Santa Fe's 56¢ tariff. While the private auto put AVI out of business, this fare increase was certainly a contributing factor.

PATRONS OF THE AVI- Freight: In later years freight held

the AVI together. The principal tonnage was sand. This, however, was a meager source of revenue. The sand haul was short, used a lot of power and, as a lower-grade shipment, carried a low tariff.

This description of a movement of sand from the sand pump south of Interurban Place to the Veterans Hospital (then under construction) confirms the economics: The AVI carried the sand to the MoPac, a distance of 7.6 miles. MoP took it about two miles to the Frisco interchange. That road then sent it to its wagon track at 17th and Oliver. Here it was loaded from gondola cars, partly by hand, into dump trucks. These trucks took it south on Oliver to Kellog and east to the construction site, where it was stockipiled on the ground for screening, batching and mixing.

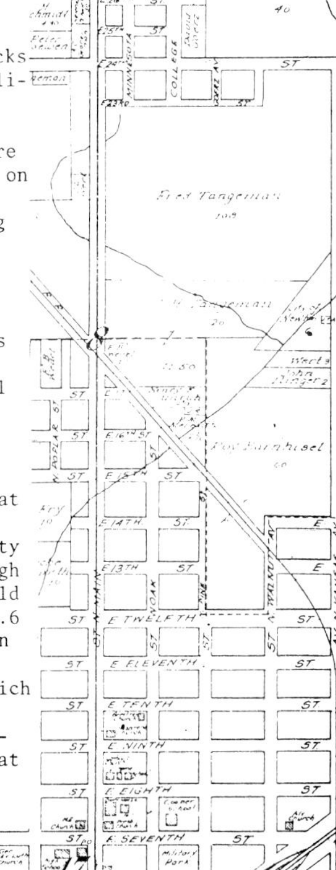

The above, incredible as it may seem in 1977, shows just how dependent society was on rail transportation in 1931!

By contrast, meat was a valuable and perishable commodity and commanded a high rate. The AVI would take fresh meat 51.6 miles to Hutchinson and transfer it to the Rock Island which would take it perhaps 206 miles further to Hooker. That would give the AVI

20% of the mileage and RI 80% (as originating carrier, AVI received a minimum of 20%). Unfortunately, most AVI hauls were short.

#602, shoving a heavy train of wet sand, dripping water from the cars, was an impressive sight, but #202, with a load of l.c.l. and two meat reefers in tow made a lot more money.

NEWTON TRACK DETAIL

This 1918 map shows how the interurban entered Newton. The Sand Creek bridge at 5th has been amended to show its shape. (This supplements the AVI map on P. 56.)

Nos. 10 and 203 stand at Wichita Freight Station in about 1921. No. 10's destination sign would indicate it was being used for both local and limited runs.

Eugene Sabin

LAST RIDE: It was a pleasant July morning.
      The rains had subsided, leaving the
air cool and the earth soaked. The cars were
meeting at Ferguson rather than at Van Arsdale
so I rode only to Valley Center. I was working the swing shift and there was no time for
a later trip.

A motor boat, with three men aboard, made
slow headway against the swollen Big Arkansas
River. Last week I could have waded it. Now
the men crouched in the boat to clear the un-
derside of the AVI trestle.

The car, as usual, left silently on authority of the conductor's hand signal. The AVI
never made much noise near the Broadview Hotel. The 3-10 series car swung around the
loop and began nosing as it attained tangent

track. The mosing continued until we reached
Valley Center.

The river was reddish-brown with mud.
Soon we crossed the Seneca St. trestle and
were running along the park-like right-of-way
near the water works, where little pools
stood in depressions in the grass. Sim Park
golf course was a study in alternate grass
and water. In some ways it resembled a swamp.

The Little Arkansas also had high water but I
saw no stranded livestock, no washed-out
bridges and no great soild erosion. Increasingly frequent rain was gradually reducing the
dust bowl and was most welcome.

Now we were speeding north away from Wichita, the air horn sounding an almost constant warning at the many grade crossings.

I thought back to a quiet summer evening
when I was about ten. I had stood among the
tall blue stem grass on the hill east of Hill-
side where I had a commanding view of the
valley and listened to an interurban running
north out of town. It made numerous stops
during which it was silent but then the
sound of gearing would come to me and pre-
sently I would hear the horn. That could
only be a passenger car over there, out of
sight, five miles away. It sounded one
note, A above middle C (the box motors had
two notes, and the locomotives three). Even
without the horn I could tell, by the frequent stops and rapid acceleration, that it
was a passenger car.

The sounds became fainter. From the direction the car must be passing Walnut Grove.
At last all I could hear was the background
rumble of the Derby oil refinery and the un-
dulating, high-pitched murmur of brake shoes
dragging on a MoP freight which was moving
very, very slowly. I had turned and walked
home. Someday I would ride the interurban,
perhaps even work for it, when I grew up.

But, as I grew up, the interurban faded
away. Now passenger service was ending and I
was not deceived by all the bold talk about
freight business taking up the slack. The
car I was riding lurched, constantly, from
side to side like a bad order amusement park
ride. The handful of people aboard were har-
dened interurban travelers who didn't mind
and who probably didn't notice. But it was
the kind of ride that would quickly sicken
those who had not ridden in recent years.
The oscillation was of constant frequency, as
long as we were moving, but increased in am-
plitude slight with speed. It was hard on
the car, hard on the track, and, while I did
not mind, it drove away passengers.

Six years ago the AVI had reclutantly laid
off all but three men of each track crew. A
succession of exteremly dry years had compen-
sated, somewhat, for the reduced track maintenance. But today the track was working up
and down, in the mud, with the passage of
each car and there wasn't enough help to level
it again before the next rain.

(Continued on P. 61)

AN INTERURBAN AT YOUR FRONT DOOR

It is now almost 40 years since the last
AVI passenger train from Hutchinson rolled to
a stop at the Wichita terminal, yet it seems
almost like yesterday. My recollection of
riding the interurban to town and back from
my home five miles north of Wichita extend
back to the early 1920s. It is difficult
for young people of today to realize the important role mass transit systems played
in everyone's life in the Teens and Twenties. There were few autos and no suburban
shopping centers. All the stores, banks
and big hotels were located in downtown
areas.

So my interest in traction developed
from the daily observation of an interurban
railway in operation by my front door. It
was fast, dependable transportation, and I
liked nothing better than to ride those big
cars. The Wichita passenger terminal was
particularly fascinating because it had
some of the atmosphere of big time railroading. Passenger, mail and express for all
points west of Hutchinson on the Rock Island
left Wichita from the AVI station, making it
seem less like short line operation. In the
middle Twenties passenger business was good,
and we never expected to find a seat when we
boarded an inbound train. The late afternoon outbound cars were always crowded but
AVI seldom put on trailers--just let the
passengers crowd on. They did try to use
the big cars (#1, #2 and #12) for these
runs, but the conductors told me it wasn't
unusual to have over 100 passengers on the
5:30 P.M. car out of Wichita.

I remember riding from Newton to Wichita
one warm summer night in 1931. My father
and I were returning from Blue Rapids, Kansas, and got off the Southern Kansas Stage
Lines bus at Newton to ride the AVI on home.
We left Newton on the last trip, about
11:30 P.M., and had to wait about 15 minutes
at Van Arsdale for the main line car to Wichita (it had been delayed at Hutchinson
waiting for a mail connection). It was
big car #2 with motorman Dan Marks, of whom
it was said he felt it didn't make any difference how late you were if you went fast
enough you were sure to get in on time. I
waded through the mail sacks and talked to
Dan as we headed south. Between Sedgwick
and Valley Center the big car was moving
fast and was really bouncing on the low
joints, so Dan would give it a little shot
of air to steady it down without taking the
controller off the brass. His estimate of
our speed was about 60 MPH. With the exception of the 1921 relocation into Wichita, the
AVI rails were laid with opposed rail joints
(both joints on the same ties). This gave
the cars an up and down bouncing motion at
speed, rather than the familiar side to
side sway produced by staggered joints.

With the Depression of the early Thirties and the advent of the auto as the main
mode of transportation, passenger business
dwindled rapidly and AVI, like many interurban lines, had to rely on freight business
to keep going. Operations became considerably more informal as l.c.l. was handled on
the passenger runs by simply removing the
seats from the smoking compartment and using

the entire front half of the car for freight.
The 10:30 a.m. trip out of Wichita carried
l.c.l. plus towing an express refrigerator
car loaded with fresh meat from Cudahy, destined for Hutchinson and points southwest
on the Rock Island. It was usually late
leaving, so passengers quickly learned to
avoid that particular trip.

The fresh meat shipments from Cudahy were
really on a tight schedule, to be loaded by
10:30 a.m. I worked a summer on the mail
desk at Cudahy in 1937, so I got quite familiar with the schedule. Cudahy salesmen
along the Rock Island west of Hutchinson
mailed their orders so they were in the Wichita main post office by 5:30 a.m. We
picked up the mail at 5:45 a.m. and had it
at the Cudahy office by 6 a.m. Orders for
Hutchinson and RI connections were marked
"AVI-9 a.m." and run through the order machines to be in the plant by 6:30 a.m.
Trucks left the plant by 9 a.m. for loading
starting by 9:15. Due to heavy volume toward
the end of the week, loading was often not
completed until after 10:30 a.m. It was a
good service for Western Kansas and Northern
Oklahome points providing next day delivery
to Liberal, Kansas; Guymon, Oklahoma, and
intermediate points on the RI.

The last big passenger movement on the AVI
involved a 3-day excursion promoted jointly
by RI and AVI, offering a round trip to Wichita from Guymon and intermediate points on
the RI for only $2.50 (this was about 1931

(Continued on P. 67)

WICHITA RAILWAY & LIGHT STREETCARS:
These photos, from Mrs. Grace Crow of
Wichita, portray three types of cars.

TOP: #190, a pre-Birney Safety Car lightweight, is shown leaving right-of-way on the
Bitting Avenue route, in verdant Riverside
Park. Motorman is Merle A. Crow. These
cars were well designed for circulation of
passengers, unlike most Wichita cars, which
disregarded this factor. One end window has
been lowered to let in the breeze, and the
wasps. The wooden slat fender, which permitted posters to be nailed to it, is typical Wichita. So is the stove, which
would usually be removed in summer. The
coke burning stove is encased in a steel
shroud topped by a 550-volt blower, seen
just behind the motorman's station. The
blower circulated air around the stove and
through a duct running the length of the
left side of the car at floor level. Ports
in the duct were baffled.

MIDDLE: Handsome car #210 heads north on
either Main or Market before double-tracking
and paving for the AVI. Brill built some
40 passenger cars like this in 1907 and
they were always used on North and South
Main. They were fast and probably were
used there because of the abundant power.

BOTTOM: Open bench car #127 is probably
on the trestle over the Little Arkansas
River on the West Riverside-Bitting
route. This appears to be a cross-bench
open converted to a rear-entrance, through
aisle type.

LAST RIDE
(Continued from P. 60)

Fifteen years ago one wouldn't have attemp-
ted to drive to Valley Center on a day like
this; the roads would have been impassible.
Today the only comfortable way to go was to
drive your own car over one of several all-
weather roads. It would cost less, too.

Valley Center came all too soon. The little agency, permanently closed with one forlorn
bench beside the door, was a sad sight. The
old rusty wye for turning rush hour cars to
Wichita was unused. The platform was built
to car floor height, so that l.c.l. and baggage could be easily brought inside. The
whole enterprise which had recently exhibited
such vitality was like an annual plant, killed
by the first frost.

Another 3-10 series car arrived from the
north. "Come aboard and we're off to the
races", said the conductor. This car rode
well; track considered. The AVI still adhered to its speedy schedule. 11.3 miles in
27 minutes may not seem fast today, but on
that track it was TOO fast. The car stopped
smoothly in Wichita. The compressor began
running. It sounded quite normal, just as if
it could go on forever; but to me it was like
the last heartbeats of a dying thing.

The handful of people aboard dispersed.
There was no one at the ticket window and no
one in any of the seats in the pleasant waiting room. I glanced down the carpeted aisle
leading from the station into the lobby of
the Hotel Broadview. In earlier times travelers and bellmen had used that passageway to
avoid the weather and to save time. The shops
at the front of the AVI building stood vacant.
Through their attractive display windows I
could see dust, litter and a step ladder.

In front of the station it was apparent
that here the double track WRR&L had become
single track and left Douglas Avenue to cross
the river on its pile trestle. In doing that
the cars had come almost to the curb and
stopped right at the station. Now this was
a Yellow Cab stand with no cab present. A
21 passenger city bus with three persons
aboard went by without stopping. Public
transportation, in Wichita, had declined almost to the vanishing point.

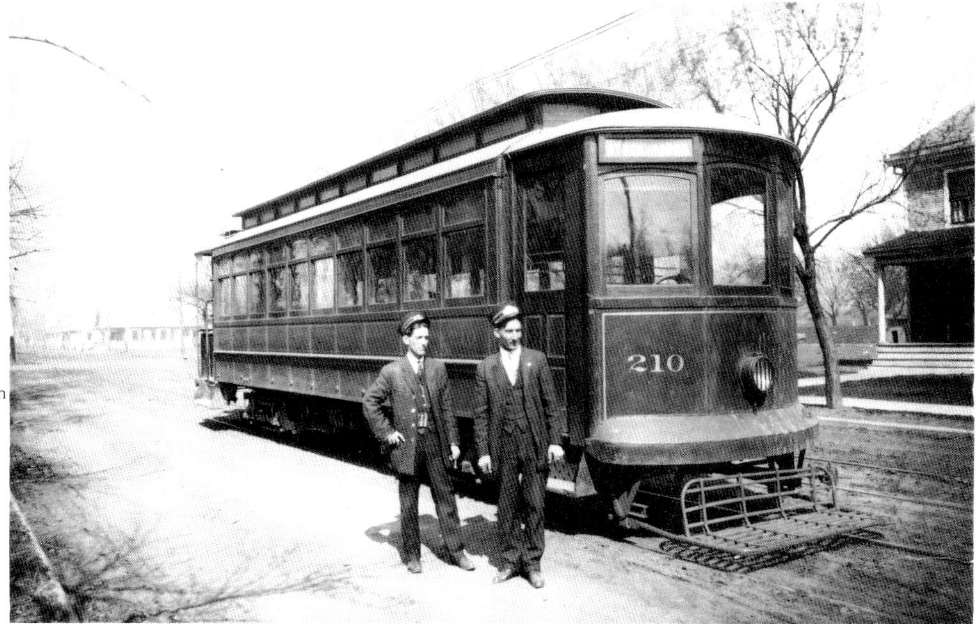

ERRATA

NOTES AND CORRECTIONS to the original material in Special 19 are based on information turned up more recently and review of the first edition.

P. 16, Paragraph 3.

The line ran in the center of Main St. (See center picture P. 16). The north end turned toward the college and was on p/r/w running east and west (see top photo P. 16). A new map in this edition will help clarify this matter. Maps are in error in that they fail to show AVI leaving 5th (in Newton) to cross Sand Creek on a pile trestle south of the wagon bridge.

P. 16, Paragraph 6. (last line)

Line to which Birney was sold was known as Union Traction Co. when the car was sold. It was changed to Union Electric Railway after its July 1935 reorganization.

P. 18, Paragraph 1.

40% of the people of the area (dust bowl) were unemployed, only about 20% of the American people were without jobs.

P. 18, Center Column, 3rd Paragraph.

Last interurban ran March 24, 1926. Last street car ran May 24, 1926. Line was dismantled Summer of 1926. In 1922 the SI obtained two large interurban cars which were sold to the Sand Springs (Oklahoma) line shortly before abandonment.

P. 20, Top Photo.

Photo shows Car 12 running south toward Wichita. (It was taken from the roof of the Sabin residence.

P. 20 Paragraph 1.

Controller designation "K" is incorrect. It was probably Westinghouse ST 37 (the 37 part is correct, since the controller had only seven points, four series and three parallel. These were the only passenger cars in Wichita with relays carried in a group box under the car. All the others had drum controllers. (AVI 602 also had this arrangement.)

P. 21, Third Column.

George Theis, Jr. was killed on August 13, 1926.

P. 22, First full Paragraph.

Campbell was not the general manager of the Wichita Transportation Corporation. He was a former official (perhaps general manager) of the Wichita Street Railway & Light Company, a predecessor of Wichita Transportation Corporation.

P. 22, Last Paragraph.

Cars 3, 4 and 5 were used on the final excursion.

P. 22 Notes on Arkansas Valley Railway Rolling Stock

Here are some roster notes:
#92 and #93 were standard General Electric products, new in 1940. Each had two 180 HP Caterpillar diesels and came from GE's Erie works. Weight: 88,000 pounds.
#91- This was a Brill gas-electric passenger car which hauled no passengers. The Salzberg management brought it to Wichita from their Southern New York R.R. It may have been used on the Vandalia Valley Ry. before that.

P. 23 , Next To Last Paragraph.

Noted Berkeley, Calif. traction historian Addison H. Laflin, Jr., commenting on the new use of the Wichita station for a radio station, said "This goes to show that you can't have your KAKE and your interurban, too."

P. 23, Upper Left Photo.

Two cars in the photo are 4 and 5.

P. 31, Car 1.

Further notes: It seated fifty. It was pulled in a train, on its own wheels, from the Jewett factory in Newark, Ohio, to Wichita.

P. 31, Car 2.

Building data on First #2 conflicts. Elmer Vallance who, as an electrician, prepared #1 and (1st)#2 for service and who, as general manager, closed down the AVI, mentioned that (1st)#2 was a Cincinnati-built car with Lorain electrical equipment and that Lorain had built the first enclosed traction motor. The 11/17/10 edition of the Wichita Eagle says that (1st)#2 came from Pullman, had no baggage compartment and seated 50 people. This story appeared after delivery and the car was presumably inspected by a reporter or by the company official who phoned in the story. The car was Pullman green and this might have caused confusion as to the builder. This car had its number changed twice and further mystery surrounds it. It was double-end and is, presumably, shown in shadow on P. 53. In this view it has no front trolley but doors at each end on the left side, implying a double-end car.

Since publication, Professor Ronald Ensz has discovered a picture postcard showing a car marked #2 and with a caption indicating that it is an AVI car at Halstead (see photo on this page). The name and logo on the car are indistinct. Truck and underbody details are clear but are obscure on our other pictures. The car has two trolleys, both raised. One is only faintly visible. The car has a baggage compartment door and the end and step details are markedly different from those shown in the picture of #01 (the third renumbering) on P. 31. Was there a (3rd)#2? The case against a (3rd)#2 follows: The car may

have been involved in an accident and the AVI chose to rebuild one end. The entire vestibule was rebuilt to AVI standards with steps of broad tread and no folding door. The other end was left as it was to protect the motorman from the weather. After that time it was usually operated as a single end car and the front trolley was, in time, removed. Also, there is no evidence other than this picture of a (3rd)#2. In rebuttal to the above: This does not explain the baggage compartment door in the car in the Ensz photograph (this page) and it would be logical for the AVI to rebuild the car as a single end car if it was planned to use it that way. On the basis of the conflicting evidence we are not prepared to venture an opinion on the existence of a 3rd Number Two. (1st)#2 became #11 when (2nd)#2 was delivered on 9/28/16. In 1921 line car #301 was damaged by fire and #11 was made into the line car (it became #01 about 1928). In 1931, line car #01 was working rail bonds and took Bell siding to let #4, an eastbound passenger car towing an empty refrigerator car, around. The helper failed to reset the switch for the main and Motorman Cliff Dancy, who was running #4, failed to notice until it was too late (he was unable to see clearly because of the morning sun in his eyes). Dancy was bruised in the collision although no one was seriously injured. #01 was scrapped and #4 was rebuilt. (The impact occured at about 30 MPH!)

Car (2nd)#2, according to the late Ira Swett's research, was built in 1915 and purchased second-hand (see text P. 31). The Wichita Eagle of 9/28/16 says it would come as a new car, from McGuire-Cummings. MUT had this car slightly over a year and it was the only car of its kind MUT had, so it may have been sent on something like a loan basis, by the builder, in hope of further business. McGuire-Cummings apparently single-ended the car for the AVI and delivered it in like-new condition. After its 1936 derailment which caused enough damage to end its career, its trucks and motors were installed, complete, under #12 in 1938, when that car was converted into an express motor.

P. 30 Lower Left Photo

The Kansas Gas & Electric locomotive has been donated to the Wichita Chapter, N.R.H.S. and is located just east of Wichita Union Station.

P. 32 Top Photo

View was taken by Eugene Sabin on the last day of passenger service, July 31, 1938. Conductor Art Spaulding is on the

(Continued on P. 63)

"

Errata (Continued from P. 62)

ground and motorman Dan Marks is at the
controls.

P. 32. Cars 3-10.

Sometime in the early Twenties all AVI
3-10 series of cars were equipped with
train air brakes. A single brake valve
controlled both straight and automatic
air (about 180° rotation. The air gauge
showed reservoir pressure and train line
pressure.

P. 33, Third Column (Individual Histories)

#4 accident was in 1931, not 1921. #6
wreck with a freight occured 7/27/30.
#7 was demotorized about 1933, and used
as a passenger trailer until about 1935,
when the body was sold and taken to a
farm near Halstead, on U.S. Hwy. 50. It was
donated to the Wichita Historical Museum in
1973 and is now at the Wichita municipal
bus barn. Last survivor of the small cars.
#10, demotorized about 1931, was used as a
passenger trailer until passenger service
was abandoned. Its body stood as a grain
storage building near 29th & Ohio until
about 1972.

P. 36, Car 201.

Car #201 was used for general box motor
duties and various construction and locomotive work until 1931 when #01 was wrecked
in a meet with #4 near Burrton. Because
of its right front door, the controls were
always on the left hand side; it being the
only car so equipped in later years. It
was also the only AVI car with a 360-degree
controller. At the time it was made a line
car it also became a two-motor car. It is
probable that it got the Baldwin trucks at
this time. The company, trying to make
ends meet, made it two-motor to save power.
After passenger service ended #201 got #8's
trucks and motors. These were 65 HP Allis-
Chalmers motors and St. Louis trucks. #201
weighed only 27½ tons instead of the 32½
ton weight of #8 and was probably the
highest performing car on the property at
the time. Eugene Sabin tells of riding
with line foreman John Erdman at 50 MPH.
Of course the wheels were now 34" rather
than 36" as it was delivered. #201's original GE 217 motors were 50 HP. The motors
used when it became a two-motor car are not
known. #217's motors could run on either
600 or 1200 volts DC. The statement that
#201 was retired in 1938 is in error.

P. 36, Car 202.

Car 202 was unable to carry 40,000 tons
of freight inside. The correct figure is
40,000 <u>pounds</u> (20 tons). The information
in the starred note (bottom of page) about
the Santa Fe overpass fails to mention
that AVI had no interchange north of the
overpass and a limited (six cars) storage
track in Newton. The overpass was a theo-
retical, not an actual, ruling grade.

P. 37, Top Photo.

Photo is by Eugene Sabin. When AVI ordered #203 the door was located at the left
because the motorman's station was, by new
AVI standard, on the right.

P. 37, Middle Photo.

Photo of 251 and 601 is looking south
from west side of the track with the 29th
St. shelter in the background. Eugene Sabin
took this, and numerous other photos in
this book, from in front of his parents'
home.

P. 37, Lower Photo.

Taken by Eugene Sabin.

AVI POTPOURRI - <u>(Upper Left)</u> AVI's Birney No. 100 heads north on Main St. in Newton. Since
it lasted so few years, ANY view is rare. (M.D. Isely Coll.) <u>(Upper Right)</u> The brick Valley Center substation, the first on AVI, is seen during construction. (Ed Tihen.) <u>(Lower
Left)</u> No. 1 is seen on the loop at Wichita passenger station about 1922-23. Note limited
destination sign. (Eugene Sabin) <u>(Lower Right)</u> Ex-AVR No. 92 became U.S. Army No. 7410,
and is seen at Ft. Holabird, Md. (P. Allen Copeland)

P. 38, Car 601.

It was built in six weeks and entered
service on 9/3/22. Photo is from the collection of Ailee Martin.

P. 38, Car 602.

The third paragraph is in error. The
640 HP rating came from a diesel salesman
who hoped to convert #602 to diesel-electric power. The GE rating was 135 HP continuous per motor (540 for four motors).
The 308 HP hourly rating per motor would
have amounted to 1,232 HP. The proposed
diesel didn't have that much power (as I
remember it was less than 500 HP) and,
because it weighed only 50 tons, the locomotive would have proved very slippery
with that much power. It might have been
able to develop that much power near the
Kansas Gas & Electric plant, which had a
total of 2,000 KW 600V power to run the
AVI and a few office building elevators
in downtown Wichita (this after 1935
when the Wichita streetcars quit). But
there wasn't enough feeder capacity to
carry this power far. None of the substations could put out this much and it
was not available at Hutchison. One
problem, not mentioned by all sources, with
the Hutchison & Northern was that the system
lacked power to move long cuts of cars. #602
was used principally to move sand from the
sand pump near Forrest Park to Wichita.

P. 39, Middle Left Photo.

Behind trailer #252 is shown one of 14 box
cars owned by the AVI. These were of 40-ton
capacity, had arch-bar trucks and rather
light draft gear. They had automatic air
brakes and were suitable for interchange,
but were never so used. Elmer Vallance said
they were bought to move wheat straw to the
short-lived Carey Strawboard plant near
Hutchinson.

P. 39, Middle Right Photo.

#3000 and #3001 are described as having
light draft gear. This is apparently a confusion with the 14 box cars in the middle
left photo note (above). These were standard refrigerator cars which regularly operated over the Rock Island from Hutchinson
to points in the Oklahoma and Texas panhandles; perhaps as far as Tucumcari, New Mexico.

P. 42, Paragraph 1.

#202-203 were never used to pull limi-
teds. They were not fast enough. Eugene
Sabin never saw either of these cars pull
a passenger trailer of any kind and neither
did the author. Note their lower gear
(high tooth) ratios on P. 36-37.

P. 49, Paragraph 3.

Hutchinson was never a meat packing center.
Those "stock yards" jointly served by the AVI
and Santa Fe, were on the order of holding
pens and chutes.

P. 49, Paragraph 4.

Some doubt that AVI owned the elevator at
Sedgwick; it was served by both AVI and Santa
Fe. Another elevator, south of Van Arsdale
was built, in 1921, by Ed Briggs and was located at Briggs siding. At the time of abandonment it belonged to J. A. Schowalter, who said
in later years that M. H. Snerson of the Arkansas Valley Railway told him the AVR was "permanent". So, he increased its capacity from
15,000 to 35,000 bushels.

P. 52, Both Photos.

Views taken by Eugene Sabin.

HUTCHINSON & NORTHERN Ry.

To the south, the Hutchinson & Southern Railway connected Hutchinson with Harper. At Harper the line connected with the Santa Fe line through the Texas panhandle and through another Santa Fe line with the Santa Fe route to the Gulf. This line was sold to the Santa Fe, which found it a valuable connecting link with its lines at Hutchinson.

Because of the success of *this* line, Hutchinson people became interested in another rail line, to the north, which would interconnect through the Missouri Pacific, Union Pacific, Rock Island and Burlington routes across the Great Plains, running east and west between points east and the Rockies.

This resulted in the formation of the Hutchison & Northern Railway Company, chartered March 21, 1912. The proposed route ran through the Kansas counties of Reno, Harvey, McPherson, Marion, Dickinson, Clay and Washington. It was to terminate at the rail junction of Fairbury, Jefferson County, Nebraska.

Headquarters were at Hutchinson and the corporate franchise ran for 50 years. The first directors were W. S. Thompson, C. O. Hitchcock, L. S. Davis, L. A. Bunker and F. E. Fearl. 1,000 shares of capital stock at $100 per share was authorized.

At the time the charter was issued Mr. Emerson Carey was serving in the Kansas Senate, representing the local district. It was through his efforts that the charter was granted to the Hutchinson gentlemen listed.

After Senator Carey completed his term of office he took an active interest in the H&N. Certain right-of-way grants were obtained in the counties mentioned in the char-

HUTCHINSON & NORTHERN RAILWAY's trio of steeple-cab electric locomotives sun themselves near the Carey Salt plant at Hutchinson. #3 is at left, #1 behind it, and #2 at right.

-David Garcia Collection-

ter, a very important one being that between property owned by the Carey Salt Co. east of the city and the Missouri Pacific RR branch line from Wichita to Geneseo, Kansas, which in turn connected with the main line of the MoPac from St. Louis, Mo., to Pueblo, Colo. (the branch also ran to a Union Pacific connection at Kanopolis, Kan.). This right-of-way paralleled switch tracks of the Santa

Fe Railway (ATSF), serving one grain elevator, Kansas State Reformatory, and the Barton Salt Co. It was thought possible that H&N might also serve those locations which would give additional service to these locations as well as any future development in the east part of Hutchinson.

Early in 1917 the Carey Salt Co. decided to move from its original location, in the center of Hutchinson, to property owned further east, outside the city limits; the new plant started operations in 1918. This plant was served by both the Santa Fe and the Rock Island railroads. The ATSF main line passed on the north the the Rock Island tracks were on the west. Outgoing shipments were from the north side of the plant and incoming shipments (such as fuel, supplies and the like) came into the south side.

In that Carey Salt was only able to make shipments of evaporated salt both the old as well as the new plant, it was necessary to ship rock salt to Hutchinson from Kansas points where rock salt mines were located, such as Lyons, Kanopolis and Little River.

Early in 1922 Carey Salt decided to sink a rock salt mine on its property approximately two miles east of the evaporating plant. The location was just south of the main line tracks of the Arkansas Valley Interurban Railway Company (AVI).

In order to move these shipments of rock salt from mine to the trunk lines, as well as the evaporating plant a method was needed. It was at this time that the Hutchinson & Northern Railway Company came into actual existence as a live railroad. Senator Carey obtained the charter from the original incorporators and formed the operating company. First officers were: Emerson Carey, President, Howard J. Carey, Vice-President, and Charles E. Carey, Secretary.

Since electric power was already being generated at the Carey evaporating plant for the Hutchinson streetcar system, it was decided to operate the H&N electrically.

Connections were planned, and made, with Santa Fe and Rock Island at tracks located south and west of the evaporating plant, and a connection were made with the AVI main line at a point known as the Carey Lake Station. An AVI connection was also made to tracks extending east of the evaporating plant. In addition, a wye track was constructed between tracks for the trunk lines and H&N tracks at the plant. Operating rights were obtained from the AVI covering the track from Carey Lake Station to a point to be known as the Carey Mine Station.

In August, 1922, construction of switch tracks, all electrified, at the mine site started and was completed in late October.

A work car was purchased from the local streetcar company to serve as a temporary locomotive over the H&N tracks, handling cars of equipment, material and the like. Due to the size of this "locomotive", only one box car could be handled at a time. Mr. Harry Stephens, the engineer, was thus the first operating employee of the company.

Early in 1923 delivery was accepted from the General Electric Co. of the first real locomotive, a 30-ton unit, Number One. It was able to handle as many as ten loads at a time in good weather. The unit operated very efficiently until business increased to the extent that it was continually overloaded, making expensive repairs necessary.

(NOTE: The Hutchinson & Northern history is an adaptation of material written by Mr. Stephen B. Horrell, who worked for the Carey Salt Company from July 5, 1921 to December 31, 1965. He participated in the conception, design, shaft-sinking, construction of Carey's three mines (besides the Hutchinson site, two others were dug at Winnfield and Cote Blanche Island, La.) He worked in the mine, ice plant and railroad, beginning as a plant engineer and retiring as Vice-President in Charge of Operations.)

A certificate of convenience and necessity allowing H&N to interchange cars with the trunk lines and the AVI was issued by the State of Kansas in July, 1923.

Late in 1923, H&N laid track and constructed overhead from its main line tracks over right-of-way obtained in 1912 to connect with the branch line of the Missouri Pacific located east of the Barton Salt Co. plant. In order to make this connection and interchange it was necessary to construct a bridge over Cow Creek as well as one over a drainage ditch east of the Reformatory. This connection gave the MoPac accesss to the industrial district east of Hutchinson as well as the AVI, through the Hutchinson & Northern.

The locomotive problem was alleviated with purchase of a 50-ton electric. It appears to have come from the St. Louis & Belleville Electric Ry., a coal-hauling freight line in Illinois. (More about it in the roster section following.) It became Number Two, and since it was designed for a higher speed than required by H&N the control was rewired to cut the speed in half. Number Two was able to handle 20 or more loads at a time. At this time Number One was used only in case of emergencies.

When the AVI quit, and was requisitioned for its track by the federal government in July 1942 (during the height of World War II), H&N purchased the portion from Carey Lake Station to the Carey Mine Station, a distance of approximately one mile. Upon this purchase the H&N was able to operate entirely on its own tracks.

An extension of H&N track was made in 1956 to the Champlin Refining Co. tank farm, located south and west of the Carey salt mine. A ten-car oil loading dock was served daily. Oil was pumped to this facility from Champlin's refinery at Enid, Oklahoma and then shipped by rail to western Kansas and eastern Colorado (some loads as far west as Denver). Rail shipments, however, were discontinued in the mid-60s due to lower trucking rates. An-

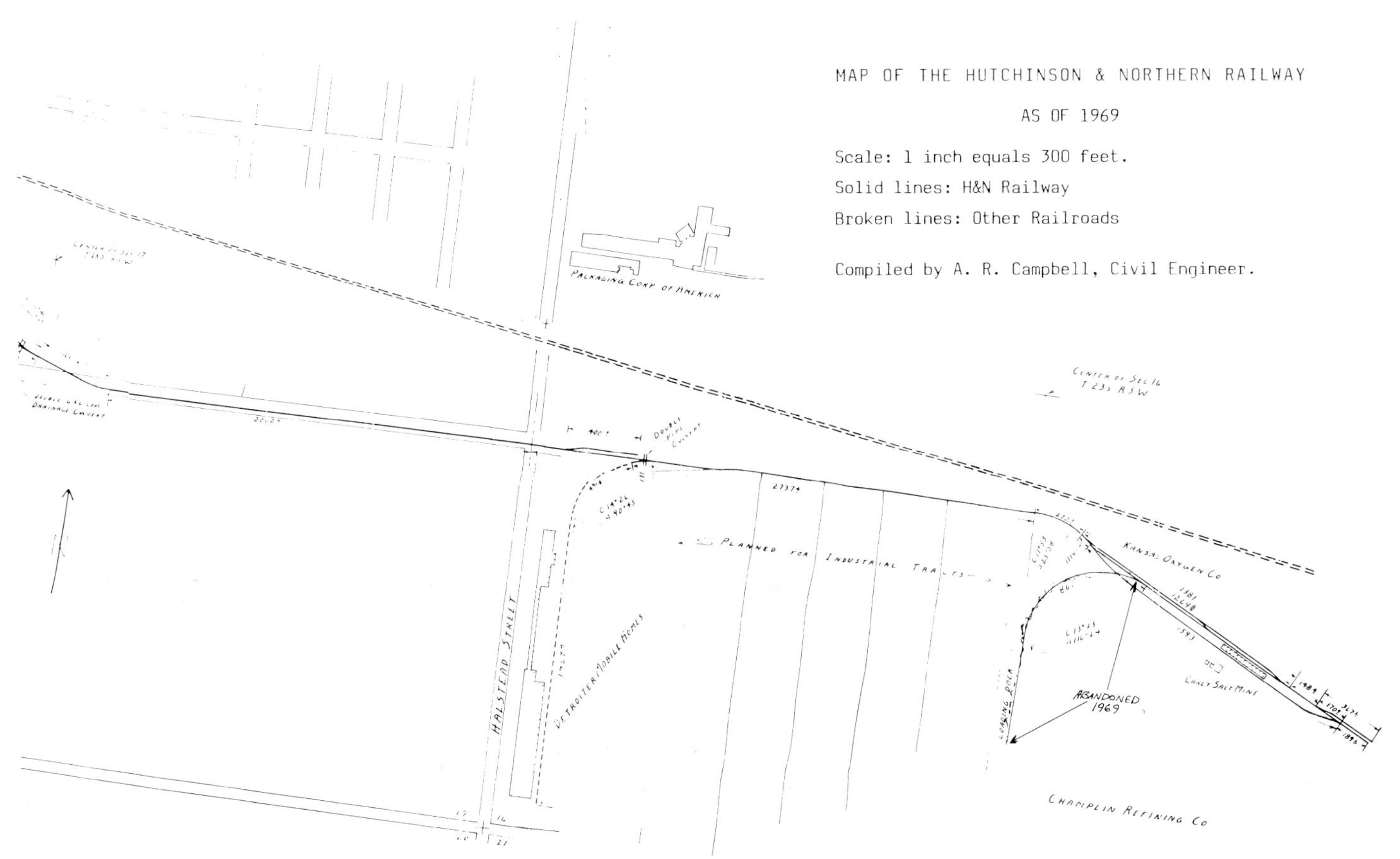

Time and wear on both Numbers One and Two were accounting for many expensive repairs by the late 1950s, and after many months of searching, a 65-ton trolley locomotive was located at the Kansas City Public Service Co., Kansas City, Mo. Built new in 1948, it was purchased by H&N in 1960. Before delivery, repainting and minor repairs were accomplished at Santa Fe Railway's Argentine, Kansas, facilities.

Number Three was in excellent condition when placed in service and its additional capacity meant work would be done in a minimum of time with safety. With controllers on both sides of the cab, the engineer was always in sight of the ground men.

By late 1963, Number Two needed major repairs, such as wheel replacement, wiring, brakes, etc., and it was decided to dispose of it. The unit was sold , and delivered by MoPac to a local iron and metal dealer. Certain parts, such as air compressor, lightning arrestors, etc. were removed for possible use on the other two locomotives.

H&N also owned six 60,000 pound capacity box cars, purchased from the Missouri Pacific in 1927. They had formerly been used on the Florence & Cripple Creek.

The company was not equipped to handle other than carload shipments. A sand loading dock was provided on a company spur and a great many cars were handled going to different highway jobs. H&N employed its own track maintenance crew and provided all tools and equipment for upkeep of track, crossings, signals, etc.

During the past few years it became necessary to construct additional storage tracks as well as replace some of the lightweight rail due to the increased car capacity limits. Whereas, in the early 1920s, 30-ton cars were quite common, 100-ton capacity cars were more the rule.

With fewer trolley locomotives in use over the nation in the 1960s and, thus demand for parts becoming less each year, parts inventories disappeared and owners had to turn to cannibalizing other units. So, all repairs were special orders, very expensive, and involving many months of delay. This also held true regarding power generating (substation) equipment. Due to these factors, management decided, in late 1969, to change to diesel electric locomotives. After making many inquiries, two 100-ton units were located at South Omaha (Nebr.) Terminal Railway. Inspection reports by factory representatives and several railroad inspectors were all favorable. Definite arrangements for purchase, including repainting, lettering and numbering, were made in late January, 1970. In February, newly-numbered Four and Five arrived at Hutchinson. All overhead fixtures , poles and other electrical fixtures were removed as of June 15, 1970.

Locomotive Number One was acquired by the Orange Empire Railway Museum, Perris, California, for preservation in 1970 and still runs there today. Number Three was sold to a private party in 1971 and was moved to the Iowa Terminal Railroad.   The diesels now operate all service on the H&N; owner Carey Salt Co. is now a division of Interpace Corporation.

HUTCHINSON & NORTHERN RAILWAY COMPANY - Locomotive Roster

No.	Type	Builder	Serial No.	Year
1	30-ton (240HP) electric	General Electric	7867	1921
2	50-ton (260HP) electric	General Electric	6988	1919
3	60-ton (400HP) electric	General Electric	29312	1948
4	660HP diesel-electric	ALCO-Gen. Electric	73353	1945
5	660HP diesel-electric	ALCO-Gen. Electric	73579	1945

Also see notes on individual locomotives on second column above

DIMINUTIVE Number One is seen in this official builder's photo at the General Electric factory. It had the look of an industrial locomotive and its most striking feature was the frameless trucks (see two views below).

Orange Empire Railway Museum Collection

Notes On Individual Locomotives:

No. 1- Built January 1921. Purchased new by H&N in September 1923. Preserved 1970 by Orange Empire Railway Museum, Perris, Cal.

No. 2- Built February 1919 for GE stock. Sold October 14, 1921, to GE's own East Erie Commercial R.R., becoming its No. 8. Sold July 1926, perhaps to the "Illinois Electric Railway", a coal hauling line from East St. Louis, Ill. to Belleville, Ill. (this has not been confirmed so it somewhat speculative), and if so, H&N bought it from that road in 1928. Sold for scrap November 1963 (still at junkyard in 1977).

No. 3- Built March 1948 for Kansas City Public Service as its No. 2. Sold to H&N in April 1959. Sold 1971 to an unknown buyer and shipped to Iowa Terminal R.R.

Nos. 4 & 5- Both ALCO model S-1, built for South Omaha Terminal Railway. (SOTR #1 became H&N #4, SOTR #4 became H&N #5.)

Traction Motors on Locomotives Numbers 1-3

No. 1- four GE 263C
No. 2- four GE 207E
No. 3- four GE 833

ARKANSAS VALLEY RAILWAY (1939-1942)

Supplemental Locomotive Data (see P. 22)

No. 91 - A gas-electric combination passenger-baggage motor (used as a locomotive on AVR). Built by J.G. Brill in 1927 (Serial No. 22590) for Lehigh & New England R.R., where it ran as No. 91. Disposition unknown.

No.s 92 and 93- Both 44-ton 380HP diesel-electrics built by General Electric new in Sept. 1940. (Serial Nos.: 92- 12912, 93-12913.) See notes for later history.

NOTES: No. 92- Sold after AVR quit to the U.S. Army, becoming #7410. Used at Ft. Knox, Ky., later at Ft. Monroe, Va. Transferred to U.S. Navy (as #7410) to Norfolk Navy Yard, Va. Sold to Beaufort & Morehead R.R. (as their #7410) at Beaufort, N.C. Sold to Cargill, Inc., Houston, Tex.

NOTES: No. 93- Sold after AVR quit to the U.S. Army, becoming #7411. Used at Army Air Force Depot, San Bernardino, Calif. Later U.S. Air Force #7411 at same location, now called Norton AFB. Sent to Hill AFB, Utah, for storage by August, 1969. Sold to Ideal Cement Co. (#029) in Superior, Nebr. (It is ironic that this expatriate from the AVI would most of its life spent switching cars received from another interurban - at Norton AFB - the Pacific Electric!)